Signs Dreams and Bullets

Lessons from a Grieving Father's Heart

Jeff M. Abbott

ISBN: 979-8-9899319-1-0

E-Book ISBN: 979-8-9899319-0-3

Audiobook ISBN: 979-8-9899319-2-7

Cover design: Miblart and Brynn O'Quinn

Artwork: Jennifer Corra, of Crescent Moon Archives

Publisher: Heartistic Publishing https://jeffmabbott.com

1st edition, February 2025

Printed in the United States of America

If you enjoyed reading 'Signs, Dreams, and Bullets,' please consider leaving a comment on Amazon or other online bookstore. Your feedback is invaluable and helps other readers discover this story.

DEDICATION

This book is dedicated to my son, Michael, who taught me so many life lessons while he was alive and even more after he passed.

CONTENTS

Acknowledgements

To all my family and friends who helped me in so many ways during this journey, and for the guidance received by Spirit on how to traverse this time. I am honored and grateful to all.

A special thank you to my writing classmates, who gave me valuable feedback as I wrote my first drafts and helped me with my manuscript.

INTRO

After my son, Michael, passed at the age of nineteen, I started writing down my experiences: the inner struggles, the questions, and most importantly, the inner dialogue between myself and the Universe. In the beginning, it wasn't my intention to write a book. Writing helped me stay focused and present, even when I wanted to turn away from things that seemed unbearable.

During this time, I didn't read any self-help books or go to counseling. Maybe that would have been helpful, but I didn't want to taint my experience or color it by trying to make it fit into a preconceived idea. This approach felt more authentic to me, a more genuine way to honor Michael and our relationship.

When you lose someone you love, it can be devastating. Your world is no longer the same. What do you do now? How do you handle it? How do you honor that person? It's a tough and painful situation, no matter how you look at it.

But through that loss, I discovered hidden there are great gifts of change and growth—an expansion of Love I didn't know existed.

Your relationship with your loved one isn't over; it can become even deeper now.

My hope is that, by sharing my experiences, I can help you connect with your authentic self and bring you closer to your loved ones and the Universe.

CHAPTER ONE

MICHAEL

It was early afternoon when Michael walked through the front door after spending the night at a friend's house. He didn't say much as he opened the fridge to get something to eat.

It was my wife who noticed and asked, "Hey, where's your car?"

When Michael didn't respond, I asked him about his car. He said he had rolled it on the freeway the night before and found himself dangling by the seatbelt, upside down in the ditch. He used his knife to cut himself free.

"Are you okay?" I asked.

"Yeah," he said.

"Oh, that's too bad about the car. It was a good one," I said. I was just glad he was okay.

"Where's the car now?"

He handed me a paper from the towing company that had hauled it away. He said the police had been there but didn't write him a ticket.

He never said exactly how it happened, only that nobody else was involved.

If he was upset or disappointed about losing his car, he didn't show it. Instead, he talked about how glad he was that he'd had his knife with him to cut himself free. Like me, Michael usually didn't make a big deal out of things and didn't complain. He had this ability to move on from situations and put a positive spin on them.

On the other hand, my wife is a worrier, and this wasn't the first time a risky situation had come up.

"Michael, you don't have nine lives," she said.

"I know, I know." He then smiled and reassured my wife. "If it's my time, it's my time, and I'll be at peace."

Anytime we'd talk to Michael about being careful, he'd say, "I know, I know."

When I saw the totaled car, I noticed that only one small area of the roof hadn't been crushed, and it was right where his head was. It was hard to believe he'd walked away without a scratch. Michael was lucky on that one. He had just turned nineteen.

Michael posted this pic with the following caption: *I really flipped my car at 80mph rolled it over 5 times and came out perfectly fine, somethin is watching over me. And thank you to the officers and first responders for showing up fast and making sure I was alright.*

This wasn't the first time Michael had a close call or that I was worried he might not make it. As a parent, I walked the line between giving him enough space and freedom to be himself and try new things, and knowing when to step in so he didn't get seriously hurt.

***

When Michael was young, he and his sister, who was one year older, were involved in lots of sports and school activities. We were always going to some event, or I was driving them to practice. Michael liked having new experiences and was curious about how things worked. He loved being silly and looking for the fun in life. He was independent, even at a young age, and not easily swayed.

Some people are followers, while others are more comfortable leading. Michael was somewhere in the middle; at times he went with the flow, and at other times he was the instigator, inviting everyone to join in.

We'd spent months looking for his first car together. Now, I'd be his ride to work until he could get another.

***

It had been a few weeks since the accident, and it was a typical summer day in Southern California. Rolling out of bed, I set my intention that morning for the day to be filled with grace and ease. I have learned over time that these intentions, when I remember to do them, have a way of being fulfilled, whether I pay attention to them or not. My job involves managing investment properties for other people, so I'm often out on appointments when I'm not working from home. As I headed out the door, the morning sun felt warm on my face. I got into my car and texted my son: "Michael, I'll be back a little later to take you to work."

The house was quiet when I came back home around noon. I dropped my keys on the counter and said hello to my daughter, Jen, who was sitting on the couch with her phone in hand. My wife was at work. There was no sign of Michael, which wasn't unusual, as he would often sleep in and get up just in time to throw on some clothes before he left. When I looked up at the clock, it was almost 1:00 p.m. *I better get Michael going*, I thought. He needed to make it to work by two.

I made my way upstairs to his bedroom to wake him up. I tapped on the door a few times and turned the handle. As soon as I opened the door, I knew something was wrong. I moved closer to the side of his bed and said, "Hey, Michael." He was lying on his side under the covers. When I moved closer, I saw that the color had already left his face. My heart quickened. I stepped into panic mode and yelled, "Oh shit!" I tried to move him to see if he was still breathing, but when I put my hand on the side of his neck, I couldn't feel a pulse. His body felt cold and stiff. He was already gone.

I heard Jen running up the stairs. I'm rarely agitated and seldom raise my voice, so she must have known something was wrong.

From there, things got a little crazy. I remember telling my daughter to call 911. Our world seemed to be collapsing in on itself.

"Is he going to be okay?" she asked.

I will never forget the look of panic, shock, and fear in her eyes.

"He's already gone," I told her.

"I don't want to be an only child!" she screamed, her face contorted. "No, no, NO!"

On the 911 call, a lady told me to start CPR. They had to follow their script, but Michael was way past that point. I started following her directions, but something told me it was no use, so I stopped. The lady on the phone kept insisting that I continue; my mind was frantic.

"I don't have time for this shit," I said and threw the phone down so I didn't have to hear her.

In a matter of minutes, our house started filling with strangers, but I stayed in Michael's room. I didn't want to leave his side.

Two paramedics from the fire department arrived first. After checking Michael, they didn't attempt CPR. As the three of us stood in his bedroom, a wave of protective parental energy welled up inside me. I'd never felt it that intensely before. It was big and powerful, flavored with anger and the need for privacy.

As calmly as I could, I said, "I know you all have a job to do, but if you don't have to be here, GET OUT!" My adrenaline was pumping, and I wasn't really asking.

They looked at each other and then left without saying a word.

Soon after, the police arrived. Two police officers very politely asked me to leave the bedroom and started taking notes and photos. They told me they had to do it because this was a potential crime scene. My mind raced. *What are they talking about?*

Then my wife called. Apparently, the telephone company had called her, saying that someone on her plan had just called 911. I couldn't say much to her other than, "Just come home, it's Michael."

When my wife walked through the door, our eyes met. "It's Michael," I said. I didn't have to say anything else.

She immediately ran upstairs, her face showing the stress and worry of receiving bad news.

When she came back down, we stood there at the bottom of the stairs with our daughter, the three of us hugging each other and crying. At that moment, I imagined a heavenly beam of light coming down from above and embracing us. There was nothing else I could do.

The house continued to fill with strangers: policemen, firemen, paramedics, a medical examiner, drivers who remove bodies. People asked questions about what had happened and told us what would happen next. Somebody handed me a flyer about grief counseling. It felt like a whirlwind inside me. As all this was going on, anger built within me. I wanted everyone to leave.

When you experience something like this, it can't get any more personal. You feel raw, vulnerable, and exposed. And the last thing you want is a bunch of strangers in your house.

Before they removed Michael's body, my wife, Jen, and I, along with our dog, Annabelle, gathered in Michael's bedroom. We said our goodbyes with lots of tears. As my wife and daughter turned to leave, I let them know I would stay a little bit longer. I put my hand on Michael's shoulder and offered a prayer honoring him. I asked that, wherever he was right now, whatever energy he needed to help him on his journey, that it go with him.

***

As you see your son's body being taken away, there's an eerie quiet that happens as everyone leaves. No one knows what to say. We are all in shock.

The house that was filled with commotion was now strangely silent. You know your family is changed forever. You're left with this empty feeling of, *Now what*? This feeling of grief, sadness, and loss envelops your whole being. I must say that the people who showed up that day were very respectful and compassionate. I don't think I would like to see the things that they see on a daily basis.

My wife and daughter are amazing, strong people, each in their own way. They've both gone through a lot. Some people, when they see others struggling, think that they're somehow weak or inadequate. My experience is that the people who struggle with things are actually the strong ones.

My wife made a request that day: that we as a family would lean in together and share whatever was going on with us. That turned out to be very good advice, as we attempted to pull together and support each other even more during that time.

Going back into Michael's bedroom a little later, I was overwhelmed by this feeling and knowing in my heart:

Oh, this is going to be hard.

CHAPTER TWO

WORDS CANNOT EXPRESS

Death has a funny way of getting you closer to life. It forces you to stop and look at what you're doing, to ask questions about what's important in life. How do you want to spend your time? Somehow, the usual distractions of the world—the things you get so caught up in—come into focus and you see them for what they are. You see your relationships from a different perspective and think about what you want to say before it's too late. (Even though it's never too late.)

A lot unravels when you lose a child. You don't sleep well, and there's a huge hole in your life. But death is a very good teacher. It can show you things in a way that are intimately personal, that cannot be told to you by another person.

***

It had been a few hours since everyone left the house. We were sitting quietly, still in shock. We had no desire to call anyone or tell anyone what had just happened, and I just wanted to be left alone. Michael was supposed to show up for work at Little Caesars, so my wife made the call to let them know that he wouldn't make it.

About an hour later, someone knocked on the front door. *Oh, great,* I thought. *Who is it now?* I opened the door to see one of Michael's friends, realizing that it hadn't taken long for the word to get out after we'd called Little Caesars. He handed me a printed photo of Michael and three of his friends having fun on a hiking trail. His friends had written notes on the photo, one of which said:

Words cannot express how truly sorry we are for your loss. Michael was our brother. Don't hesitate to reach out if you need anything.

"Thanks, I really appreciate it," I said.

I was impressed. Here was this young guy, coming to our door, doing something way beyond his years. He was straightforward, honest, and respectful with his words. All I knew at that point was that these guys had a genuinely deep connection—the kind that's forged through lots of history, good and bad, and going through tough times together. The authenticity showed on his face.

He wouldn't be the only one of Michael's friends who would come to our door and share how they felt, some of whom we'd never even met. It spoke to how much Michael meant to them and showed me just how deeply Michael's life had impacted so many others. His friends were truly his second family.

That photo is still hanging on our refrigerator.

Chapter Three

I Got This

The medical examiner told us that it would take between four to six months to determine Michael's cause of death. Covid-19 was taking its toll, and everything was backlogged. I had a pretty good idea about what had happened, but I didn't want to tell anyone. Still, we knew people would ask.

"What are we going to tell people when they ask what happened?" my wife asked.

She had the point of view that it was none of their business.

"We'll tell people that we don't know yet, because that's the truth," I said.

Later, we found out that Michael had taken something laced with fentanyl, which had stopped his breathing. Michael had been struggling with drugs and addiction for a while. We had tried individual counseling, group sessions, and cold-turkey isolation methods through hospitals, but nothing worked. Although I believe he did benefit from these interventions, he hadn't made the decision for himself to quit, and no one can make it for you. Michael wasn't one to be swayed or convinced about something unless he chose it for himself.

The counselors often told us that Michael was unique, in his insights and in his approach to life. He had a center that did not waver. Although they couldn't divulge specifics, the counselors told us that they liked what Michael brought to their sessions.

I often asked myself, *What does Michael need?* One answer that came up was that he just needed more time—time to become more of who he was.

My wife recounted a conversation she'd had with Michael about using drugs. At first, he said that drugs gave him experiences that were mind-expanding and fun. He researched each drug, calculated how much to take, and figured out what to mix it with or not. He said he was in control. He was never one to complain and would often say, "I got this," when any risky situation came up. He said, "I got this," so many times that I made a poster showing him skiing down the steep slopes of Mount Shasta saying those words.

Michael's Poster

When my wife would tell Michael to be careful, he would say, "Don't worry, Mom. I got this." When he said, "I don't got this," one day, we knew he was struggling, but most people wouldn't have known it by speaking with him.

Sometimes Michael talked about how we don't know how long we have here on Earth. He'd say, "You know, life is short." He seemed to have a sense that he wouldn't be here long, or at least that there was no guarantee. As a parent, that was hard to hear.

It's difficult to watch as you see where your child's path may lead. It causes you to hold your breath. You try to help your kids by giving them the tools they'll need to handle different situations along their journey. It's a balance of knowing when to be tough and when to give them enough space to choose and make their own mistakes. Ultimately, you recognize that you don't really have any control over their choices.

***

In our living room, my wife, daughter, and I tried to piece together what had just happened and what events led to all this.

The night before Michael passed, Jen and he had been playing video games in the living room. At 1:00 a.m., Michael got a phone call. The name didn't show up on his caller ID, so it must have been someone he didn't usually talk to. After a short conversation, he told his sister that he was going out.

Michael returned home at 4:00 a.m., when my wife was already getting ready for work. Since Michael was upbeat and talkative before going to bed, she didn't check on him before she left.

***

My wife decided to call whomever he'd met the night before to make sure they hadn't taken any drugs—or if they *were* taking drugs at that time, not to use them, since we didn't know what had caused Michael's death. We wanted to give them a heads-up and hopefully find out some information about Michael, too.

She tracked down their phone number and made the call. When a girl answered, my wife introduced herself, then let her know that Michael had passed away the night before. The girl was in shock. My wife told her to be careful if any drugs were involved, but it turned out their meeting didn't have anything to do with drugs. She said if there was anything she could do, to let her know. I was surprised at how openly the conversation flowed.

The girl was a friend of his from high school and had reached out for somebody to talk to. Michael had an open heart, especially for those who were going through a rough patch. He and the girl had met somewhere near the beach to talk.

My wife texted her later, asking if she would be willing to share anything about Michael's state of mind that night. This was the text message my wife received:

When I was with him he was discussing life and things he planned to do, like getting his uncle's car and moving into a place with his friends. He told me a little bit about his family history and how you grew up on a farm in Japan. He didn't seem depressed. He was happy and was giving me advice while I was sad. He did tell me about some of his drug problems, highlighting the fact that no matter what someone says or does to stop him he would find a way to get what he wants. He was also excited about the paycheck he was getting at his new job. Telling me how he set aside $400 for a new car, giving it to his sister to hold for him. I asked him how he got his first car. This ties into you coming from Japan, how you guys worked for *everything you have and he wanted to do the same. How when he was little he was given a 25 cents allowance, then a savings account and that's how he bought his first car.*

When I read this text message, it confirmed what I'd thought: Michael hadn't attempted to commit suicide.

Later on, she attended Michael's celebration of life and shared more about their time together that evening. Michael was being silly and trying to make her laugh—something that a good friend would do. When she mentioned she was getting hungry, Michael said he would jump into the water and get them a crab to eat. I can picture Michael saying this with a grin on his face, knowing he would actually jump in the ocean and try to do it.

She also sent us a picture of a tattoo she got in remembrance of Michael. The words go across her back, from shoulder to shoulder: "Until we meet again." There's a living hand on one side and a skeleton hand on the other, almost touching each other in the middle. In the center is a dagger with butterfly wings.

When I saw this tattoo, it made me realize how much Michael meant to her. I thought, *If that's not making an impact on someone's life, I'm not sure what is.* It was another way to show me how much Michael meant to so many people.

Tattoo

CHAPTER FOUR

A MESSAGE

I often receive insights and intuition about situations, glimpses of what's going to happen. It's deeper than just thinking about something; instead, it drops in like a deep knowing. I refer to these messages as "downloads." The day after Michael passed, while I was sitting by myself on the couch, I received one of these downloads. It came in loud and clear.

Okay, now you can have a deeper relationship with Michael. You have the idea that this loss will make things harder, separate, and more distant. But, actually, you can now be even closer, more fully there, and more intimate with Michael.

Spirit has a way of communicating the truth with you, even if your mind rejects it or can't see how it could happen.

Over time, I've learned to trust these messages, or at least be open to them, even when I'm shown something out of the ordinary.

As I heard this message, I felt a sense of excitement and nervous anticipation: excited because something beautiful was about to open up that would allow me to have something new, and nervous because I wasn't exactly sure how it would unfold or what it would look like. I knew this was a precursor for a change about to happen.

My mind kicked in at the same time with its doubts, questions, and judgments:

That doesn't make any sense.

How's that going to happen?

That's going to be tough when he's not even here.

It wasn't until much later that I understood what this message meant.

***

Inner World

Your inner world, those private thoughts and feelings you think no one else can see, feels like you're the only one experiencing them, or at least that's what we believe. It's the space where you feel the most intensely, whether the feelings are good or bad. It's your inner world, when you're injured or hurt, that needs healing. No one else can reach in there and magically fix something—at least, not without your permission. Yet true healing happens in this inner space. It's the place where you experience the most intimate connection with yourself.

Amazing transformations can happen instantaneously in this inner world through a realization, a divine inspiration, or a decision. The outside world might see an amazing transformation and ask how you could change so quickly, but for you the change has already happened inside, and it's just a reflection of what has already happened. For me, this inner change matters the most—becoming more whole, more at peace within myself. It's a sense of freedom and connectedness with who I am. This is an internal journey, and the outcome of what happens in the outer world comes in a distant second place.

My tools in this world are the intentions I make and the questions I ask. The more authentic and raw I am with myself, the more honest I am, the more powerful I can be in the inner world.

Another tool I have is my willingness to be open to whatever shows up, to be in a receiving space and okay with not knowing the answer, to step into the unknown and see whatever is there. I am often surprised by what I find, discovering beauty, resilience, and love.

Chapter Five

When Everybody Comes

Over the next few days, as more people found out that Michael had passed, they came to our house, some bringing food. I was surprised when even neighbors we didn't know well stopped by. This was nice and touching; but I also found it to be difficult.

It can be awkward to be around certain people while you're grieving. Some people want to reach out and be supportive, but they aren't sure what to say or even if you want to talk. Others avoid you, or at least avoid what your grief brings up within them.

I wanted my space. I didn't want to be asked how Michael died—and relive the grief of that moment—to satisfy someone's curiosity. Actually, I wasn't too concerned about the why. The details of what happened didn't really matter to me, because it wouldn't change anything. I know my wife and daughter felt the same.

Whenever the doorbell rang, I was the one who answered it, as my wife and daughter didn't want to. I often felt a tightness around my throat when I was at the door, fighting back tears as people offered their condolences. Other times, I was just numb, with no reaction at all to what they said.

Some people offered advice. I would hear things like, "You just gotta keep going," "Just stuff everything down if you have to," and, "This is the kind of thing that will never go away for you." Some people, even if they didn't directly say it, were thinking, *I'm glad this didn't happen to me.* Some were just genuinely sad, and though they didn't know what to say or do, they still wanted to be there.

The most awkward situation, the one that rubbed me the wrong way, came with the feeling of, "Oh, I'm so sorry for you. You must be feeling terrible. You must be so down." It was a form of pity. It felt like heavy syrup being poured over me. This did nothing to bolster my feelings and just brought my attention to sadness and grief. Along with it came a kind of hidden judgment, that it wasn't okay for me to be where I was. It focused on a perceived weakness instead of the strength of who I am.

Even though I appreciated the motivations behind these suggestions, none of them resonated with me. In the end, I would thank the person for coming, sometimes shrugging my shoulders and putting my hands up, saying, "There's not really anything anyone can say." There's no instruction booklet on how to help a grieving person, and sometimes it's difficult to share what you need or want to happen.

For me, I wanted to feel connected with my family and also with Michael, to see where he's at now. This desire to connect with Michael was the beginning of my healing journey, which unfolded in ways I never expected. I didn't want to put his death in a category or to reframe it just so I could feel better. I wanted to experience it directly for myself.

***

When someone close to you dies, the people around you offer a mixed bag. On the one hand, it's nice to hear how much your loved one meant to them and how much they cared. On the other hand, people bring you all their sadness, all their ideas about death, all their fears, questions, and projections about what happened. Even if they don't say a word to you directly, their energy will add to what you're already going through.

Other people in my situation might have wanted to be surrounded by friends, but that wasn't what I wanted, at least not in the beginning. I just wanted to be left alone, to give myself space to breathe and process what was going on.

I think what I really needed was to know that I was seen. I wasn't necessarily looking for a fix. I couldn't just fast-forward to the end of the video and suddenly be better.

The most helpful people at that time were the ones who recognized and honored the loss they'd experienced within themselves. They owned where they were and didn't try to put anything on me, minimize what had happened, or tell me to feel better. They let me know that they were there with me, focusing not so much on the grief but on the love and the relationship they'd had with Michael. They kept things short and sweet (like Michael's friends who came to the door), just a couple sentences letting us know they were there, but they didn't prod or impose their judgments and beliefs on the situation.

Sharing loss in this way feels authentic to me. Maybe that's why, during this time, we were able to pull closer together as a family. We all shared that loss.

After having more time to reflect, I can see everyone's good intentions, no matter how they came across to me. I now appreciate even more the cards and messages of support from everyone who came to offer condolences.

CHAPTER SIX

A TRAP

The weeks following Michael's passing were especially tough: Waking up in the middle of the night crying. Wrestling with feelings of grief, loss, sadness, and anger. Feeling like I'd totally failed Michael as a father. *Maybe if I had done something different or shared more of myself with him,* I thought, *he might still be here.* These emotions often surfaced at the most inopportune times. I really didn't have control over them.

Rather than distracting myself or avoiding any triggers, I tried my best to let those images and memories play out. I didn't try to push them away, deny them, or change them, but instead allowed them to run their course. I wasn't always successful. Memories and emotions are powerful and can take you over if you let them.

My wife and daughter each grieved in their own ways. Sometimes, early in the morning, my wife and I would sit and discuss funeral arrangements, what we needed to do next, and any feelings that were coming up. My wife, who works with cancer patients, selectively reached out to the people she knew were capable of hearing her grief. Jen went to counseling, made collages, and wore Michael's hoodie. We often talked about Michael; it wasn't a taboo subject for us.

I noticed I had this idea that if I didn't always feel an intense emotion surrounding Michael's passing, it somehow meant I didn't love him. I knew this wasn't true. Eventually, I saw this as a trap, and I knew that if I allowed this belief to stay, I would be prone to reliving certain memories, stuck in a loop like an addict. Once I saw this trap for what it was—just a belief—it was easier to release my hold on it. I didn't have to prove to myself that I loved Michael, and it wasn't necessary to hang onto the intensity.

***

Michael was constantly using my tools in the garage to build things. He liked to make his own guns, knives, crossbows, and swords, and he was curious about how they worked. When Michael was younger and we went on hikes together, he would find sticks and feathers, bring them home, and make bows and arrows out of them. He spent hours and hours working on projects and figuring out how to make a trigger mechanism work. He had a lot of patience with his interests and would be a great guy to have along if you needed someone with survival skills.

I grew up in a family with guns in the house, and it wasn't a big deal. We were taught to treat them with respect. Michael was always safety-conscious, but the combination of his being under the influence and having weapons around made me nervous. Earlier, I'd tried taking away things that were dangerous, but I quickly realized it was a losing battle. Michael had this enthusiasm, excitement, and commitment toward his projects, and as he got older, his "projects" became more advanced, so instead I took on the role of safety advisor. That seemed to work a little better, and I'm sure I prevented some disasters.

If any of his projects were going to explode, Michael would ask my permission first. He was respectful. After inspecting what he was doing, along with ensuring that he had the necessary hearing protection and goggles, I usually said okay. But I still worried about the human factor, the potential mistakes and accidents.

One evening, I was sitting on the couch when the front door opened and Michael walked in, having come home after testing one of his projects. He was holding his hand, which was wrapped in a red-stained paper towel.

"What happened to your hand?" I asked.

"Oh, it's nothing."

I stood up from the couch. "Here, let me take a look." He still had all his fingers, but there were some deep wounds.

"The alignment of the chamber and the barrel was off," Michael said. The shell had exploded out the side of the gun and into his hand.

"Can you still move your hand?"

"Yeah."

"Let's get this cleaned up."

I pulled out a strong magnet from the kitchen drawer and moved it over the surface of his skin, trying to remove any metal shrapnel that may have been in there. The tone of our conversation was calm and matter-of-fact.

I smiled. "You gotta be careful."

"I know, I know."

"This one could have been bad. You're lucky it blew out the side and not straight back into your face."

"Yeah, I know."

I got some bandages and antibiotics and wrapped his hand.

"We'll check it in the morning. If it looks like it's getting infected or isn't healing, we'll go to the doctor."

The next morning, when I told my wife what had happened, she was worried, of course, but she mostly just shook her head. This wasn't out of the ordinary.

Later, Michael posted a pic of his hand on social media with the following caption: *don't play with guns. down to the bone. not discouraged tho.*

We ended up taking Michael to the doctor to have him checked out. Luckily, there was no serious damage.

***

It's Not Okay

Being forced to let go is scary. The change is abrupt, chaotic, erratic, and shaky. While it's happening, it feels like there isn't anything stable to hang on to, and it makes no sense.

Coming across Michael's old, partially finished projects in the garage brought back some good memories of us doing things together. It also reminded me how often I'd kept an eye out for situations moving toward that tipping point of no return, especially during the last year of his life. It's normal for parents to worry about their kids, but outcomes that could lead to their death are more intense than not making the sports team, failing a test, or not getting into a chosen college. I worried about receiving a call from his friends, school, or the police that he was hurt, or that he had accidentally hurt someone else. Michael, of course, wasn't worried about any of this and continued being himself—a free spirit.

Now that Michael had passed, the stressed part of me felt relief, followed by a sense of guilt. This judgment arose and told me, *It's not okay. You shouldn't feel anything good about your son's death. It's supposed to be sad.* Feeling relief felt like it somehow diminished my relationship with Michael.

I took a deeper look at this judgment, reflecting on what it told me. I recognized that this judgment depended on what my relationship with Michael was based. If our relationship was based on fear and worry, then yes, it was diminished. But if it was based on something else, something more permanent, what I would call "real," then as worry and stress moved aside, there would be more room for something deeper to take its place, to fill in with what was already there.

***

Questions

I had a lot of questions after Michael passed: *Is he okay? Where is he? Where do we go from here?* I noticed my mind trying to attach stress and worry to these questions. It was interesting to see how stress and worry try to continue, like they have a life of their own, and how my mind tried to go back to what was familiar, only in a different form. I saw that the thoughts based on worry and fear didn't benefit Michael or me; they only led to more of the same. So I tried not to put energy into them.

My questions about Michael didn't go away, but I began shifting away from fear and worry and asking those same questions from an authentic space of inquiry—from an open-hearted, childlike space of simply wanting to know. I was purely looking to see what was there, with no expectations or predefined answers.

Respect, honesty, and acceptance are already present when asking questions from this space. I found doing so honored both Michael and myself. This was key for me to be open to receiving something new.

CHAPTER SEVEN

EXPERIENCE WITH DEATH

Loss pushes us to the edge. It brings out the things we often don't want to—or are unable to—see that are right in front of us. If and when we're ready, loss allows us to meet what is being brought forward with who we truly are; and the more of ourselves we bring to the situation, the more easily we can be with it, to see it for what it is. In the same way, the smaller we think we are, and the more divided we feel about ourselves, the more complicated life becomes. The beautiful thing is that when our experience is whole and all is included, we can honor everything that loss brings forth. Love allows us the freedom to embrace all that life has to offer, and to give whatever is needed to the situation.

Only you can know what is needed when you're moving through loss. No one else can tell you, for no one has your life or your experiences.

***

My first direct experience with death was with our dog Tripper, a beautiful yellow lab with a gentle, upbeat personality. We took him to the vet when we noticed him struggling, and it turned out he had a condition that restricted his breathing. Not much could be done, and if we did nothing, he would slowly die of asphyxiation. My wife and I discussed what to do. How would we decide what was the right thing to do and when? Why were we keeping Tripper alive—because he was experiencing a great quality of life, or because of our own desire to have him with us? We made the hard choice to have him put to sleep.

The vet came over to our home—a blessing in those days, as veterinarians didn't often make house calls. In our garage, as Tripper lay on his padded blanket and we sat on the floor next to him, his eyes still had the glint of a happy dog, yet he looked tired at the same time. Some might think that it's easier to know when death will happen, but I don't think so. We said our goodbyes, then the vet made the injection.

What I experienced next surprised me. When Tripper's body relaxed, I saw his essence/spirit leave his body. It moved upward and seemed to pause for a moment about six feet above us. I felt a sense of complete joy, of gratitude for all the times we had spent together. In a strange way, it was beautiful. I didn't share this with my family right away, as they were having their own experience with Tripper.

I experienced something similar with my mom, who passed away a few years ago. After she passed, I sent her an internal hello, and I got a sense about where she was—a place of pure peace and contentment. She was happy. I experienced this as a knowing within myself that needed no explanation. It just was. It's more difficult to feel sad when you *know* a person is happy and not just because you're hoping it's true.

My brother Rob's passing, which happened about five months before Michael's, was different. He had been in the hospital battling an array of things, and eventually his body got to the point where it was unable to continue. Adding Covid-19 to the situation didn't help. Our family is spread out from Japan to the Midwest, and since I lived in the same city as my brother, I was the doctors' main contact person. I kept my phone turned on all night, as the doctors would sometimes call us late at night asking permission to do procedures. Those calls were never good news, and the doctor's voice would often sound urgent and tinged with panic—like if we didn't take action now, the outcome wouldn't be good. Needless to say, this was stressful, especially when my brother was walking that fine line between life and death.

The night before he passed, I was working at my desk at home. Rob and I had a business together, and because I was covering all his clients while he was in the hospital, I was burning the candle at both ends. At 10:00 p.m., I felt Rob's presence. As I looked up from the screen, he was there, on my right side a little above my shoulder. I saw his face clearly. I said out loud to him, "Oh, hi, Rob." I was surprised to see him, but at the same time, it felt like the most natural thing in the world.

The rest of the conversation didn't involve any spoken words. They weren't necessary. I could feel him there, letting me know that he was totally at peace and fulfilled. At that moment, if anyone had asked me if Rob needed anything, I would have had to say no.

The very next morning after Rob's evening visit, I received another call from the doctors saying that Rob had taken a turn for the worse. They had tried to remove the ventilator, and it hadn't gone well. They said, "If you want to come to the hospital, now would be a good time."

When my wife and I arrived at the hospital, the emergency Covid ward looked like something out of a TV show. Multiple rooms were taped off and covered in sheets of plastic with special filter systems in place. Some doctors were wearing what looked like hazmat suits as they moved from room to room, and the sounds of beeping monitors filled the hallway. We stood just outside Rob's room, looking through a glass panel that allowed us to see him without going in. He wasn't conscious; my sense when I saw him was that he wasn't really there.

I asked the doctor, "What's the next course of action? What's the prognosis?"

The doctor took a long pause. I could tell he was trying to figure out the best way to tell me, but that pause told me everything I needed to know. He didn't have to say anything more. There was nothing that they could do at that point. Only the machines were keeping his body alive.

Our focus shifted from a path toward recovery to what we could do to make him as comfortable as possible. With tears, my wife and I said our goodbyes through the glass. If Rob hadn't visited me the night before, it would have made a difficult situation even more difficult. A few minutes later, he passed.

My son's passing at the age of nineteen a few months after that was a lot harder. Unresolved conflicts, which had been lying dormant within me, were brought to the surface.

CHAPTER EIGHT

SHARING WHAT YOU LOVE

Every relationship is unique, and Michael's and my wife's was no exception. My wife showed her love by making the foods he liked, and when she was at Michael's soccer games, swim meets, and wrestling matches, you could hear her yelling, "Come on, Michael! Come on, Michael!"

She's an organizer and likes having things in their place. If we're going on a trip, it's not unusual to see the suitcases lying on the bedroom floor weeks in advance. Michael, on the other hand, tended not to overthink, having an attitude of, "Let's just go do this and see what happens."

Whenever Michael and my wife disagreed on how to do something, it was never mean. It wasn't a question of whether they cared about each other. Michael knew his mom loved him. But they were different people, and sometimes it was comical—at least for me—how it played out.

***

Michael loved watching YouTube videos and would be excited to share what he discovered. Sometimes it was a video about, as Michael would say, "Stupid things people were doing," or it was a new gun being made and tested.

My wife was making lunch one day when Michael walked up and said, "Hey, Mom, take a look at this."

My wife stopped what she was doing to look at the video playing on his phone. With a sparkle in his eyes, Michael said, "Look at this new type of bullet," and went on to explain what they were doing and how they tested it.

My wife watched with a confused look on her face, trying to figure out what she was seeing. She has zero interest in anything related to guns, and after a few moments, she said, "Michael, I don't know what this is. I don't understand."

"I know, I know, Mom, but just look. See how this new type of bullet can go through metal."

At the end of the video, they paused and looked at each other. Not really knowing what else to say, Michael smiled, my wife smiled, they both said, "Okay," and then Michael walked away.

I found it both funny and beautiful that they had these types of conversations. Even though my wife didn't understand what Michael was talking about, it didn't matter as long as he could share something he loved and was excited about.

When someone shares what they love with you, even if you don't understand it, it shows a lot about how they feel about you.

***

Saying that Michael and my wife had different styles of cleanliness and neatness would be an understatement.

When Michael was younger, we tried many approaches to get him to clean up after himself. Sometimes, we hoped a simple reminder would do it. He would say, "Yeah, I'll do it," and then he wouldn't. Other times, we tried rewards or consequences, but consequences only work if the person cares about them, and Michael didn't have a lot of attachments. I'm sure most of you who have teenagers can relate when I say they can have a strong will.

My wife would often pre-make meals for us and keep them in the fridge, as everyone in our family had their own schedules. After Michael made himself something to eat, he would often leave the dishes on the dining room table. Sometimes my wife or I cleaned off the table, sometimes Michael would. This was just how things were. It was an ongoing battle, usually between my wife and son. They never yelled at each other, but my wife quietly fumed, so it was always interesting to me to see how it was going to play out.

One day, Michael made himself lunch by grabbing whatever he could find out of the fridge, and he also had a large plate full of mangoes, bananas, and blueberries. He ate at the dining room table while watching videos on his phone. A little later, I heard my wife ask Michael to come clean up and put the dishes in the dishwasher, and he gave the usual response: "Okay, okay, Mom."

The next day, I noticed the dishes were still on the table, with a partially eaten sandwich and some fruit still on the plate. I thought to myself, *Looks like my wife is going to hold out for a while on this one.*

Another day went by, and my wife was still holding out. The fruit flies had discovered this wonderful treat and were buzzing around in endless circles above the plate, yet my wife still didn't take the dishes away. Without even bothering to shoo away the flies, she put plastic wrap over the top of the plate, covering everything—fruit flies and all. Michael would still say, "Okay, okay," when asked to clean up. I decided to stay out of this one.

On day four, I walked into the dining room. The fruit had turned interesting colors, and the fruit fly swarm had invited all their friends to the party. Despite the plastic wrap, they managed to find a way in and seemed quite happy as they enjoyed their free meal. I smiled and decided to check in on Michael, who was sitting on the living room floor playing a video game. I tried to keep it light.

"Michael, are you growing a fruit fly farm over there?" I asked.

He looked up and smiled. "I don't know."

I nodded my head and walked away with a knowing smile.

Looking back, my wife and I laugh about this. They were both stubborn, and, in the end, Michael won this one; my wife ended up cleaning the dishes. I'm sure Michael got a laugh out of that, with a big grin on his face.

***

My wife is a worrier, but before Michael passed, she told me she decided for herself not to hold back and to just do what she wanted in her relationship with Michael. If she felt like giving him a hug, she did. If she wanted to tell him not to get sick with Covid, she did. When she worried about his safety, which was often, she'd tell him to be careful. Michael's response was usually, "Okay, okay," even if he disagreed. Sometimes he would say, "If it's my time, it's my time, and I'll be at peace."

Michael didn't always get where she was coming from, because that's not how he was. He went with the flow and believed that things in life worked out.

Having done what she'd wanted to do helped my wife handle Michael's passing. She didn't have as many regrets because of that, and she adopted the idea that when it's your time to go, it's your time to go.

***

My wife would ask me what I saw in Michael's future—not what I thought, but what I intuitively saw. But I couldn't see anything when I looked at Michael. I would check several times and get nothing. This bothered my wife, because I could see what my daughter looked like and where she was, but it was a blank for Michael. My wife asked me why I couldn't see Michael, and I said maybe because Michael hadn't made the choice yet.

A few months before he passed, that changed. I could see something there. It showed itself to me as a pathway that went horizontal for a long time, but then went vertical and opened up. Seeing this showed me that at least there was a way, a way that was possible.

I often asked myself what Michael needed, how I could help. Sometimes the answer was support, sometimes something else, but the last answer I received when I asked was that Michael just needed more time to go through the things he needed to experience and then the vertical part of the journey would happen. In my mind, this would occur in about three to five years. This was different, because before there was no line, no path. So when Michael passed, I knew right away that this wasn't suicide; it was an accidental overdose.

May those who have lost someone to drugs be comforted and supported.

Chapter Nine

What Is Meant for You

I didn't feel much like working after Michael passed. The good thing about being self-employed is that there's no one telling you that you have to go to work or be at the office at a certain time. The bad thing is that no one tells you that you have to go to work.

On the scale of life, work seemed so insignificant. I was riding waves of sadness, loss, and grief, and when these emotions came, they were front and center in my world.

***

One morning, instead of doing work, I decided to go to the beach. I find the ocean comforting. Looking out at the horizon over the water gives me a sense of calm. The waves sometimes crash in, sometimes gently lap against the shore, but no matter what's happening with the waves, the horizon line is big, wide, and open. I love the ocean breeze and the whiff of salt air, and the sounds of the waves as they come in with a roar, crash in on themselves, and then finally, gently roll onto the shore in the final few feet of their journey.

The sun was shining as I made my way down the sandy beach toward the water. I found a good spot and made a place to sit in the sand. The great thing about sand is that you can shape it into anything you want—within reason—and make it a comfortable place for yourself.

Other people were walking on the beach: couples, moms with kids. I wondered how their lives were unfolding, all the choices they were making, and what they were experiencing. I wondered if they realized how lucky they were to share that time with each other.

As I looked toward the horizon, my mind began to follow my emotions. I felt a sense of loss with some regret poured over the top. I thought, *Maybe if I had been a better dad, maybe if I had given more of myself...* I regretted all the words I thought I could have or should have said, missed the milestones that Michael was not going to reach: getting married, discovering his own path, having kids. I missed all the experiences we could have shared together, however they would've played out. This is a dangerous road to go down, for it leads nowhere. But my mind attached its own meanings to these feelings as they came up. It told me that I was missing out.

Sometimes, you just have to let your mind go, and you have to let yourself cry. Feel the emotions in your body and allow them to run their course, full force, with no restrictions. So that's what I did.

After about an hour, the tears seemed to have run their course. My T-shirt was wet with sweat, but the waves were still coming in and gently lapping against the shore. The seagulls were squawking and flying overhead. I was still sitting in my spot in the sand.

As I stood up, my body felt a little stiff, possibly from not moving or just because I was getting older. I headed toward the boardwalk that runs along the beach where most people were walking, riding their bikes, or jogging, with vendors selling trinkets, jewelry, and souvenirs. As I slowly made my way down the boardwalk, someone behind me yelled, "Excuse me, would you like to have some happy thoughts?"

I wasn't sure the voice was addressing me, so I kept walking and didn't turn around. "Excuse me, would you like to have some happy thoughts?" they yelled again.

This time, I turned around. It was a young woman in her mid-twenties standing off to the side in the grass with a bright smile. Next to her were a small chair and a square folding table. What looked like colorful hoodies and bags were spread out on the grass.

As our eyes met, she asked again, "Would you like to have some happy thoughts?"

I paused for a second and then said, "Sure."

Who wouldn't like some happy thoughts? I said to myself.

As I walked over, I wondered what she meant by that, but in the back of my mind, I was wondering what she would try to sell me.

She motioned to the table and said, "Here, pick one out."

On the table, many small colored envelopes were spread out in piles.

"How much is it?" I asked.

"Oh, these are free."

I took a quick look at her to see if she was telling the truth. Then I reached down, picked up one of the envelopes, and opened it. Inside was a handwritten card. It read:

"There isn't a thing in this world that can take what is meant for you."

After I read this, I saw and felt the meaning of these words for me.

There isn't a thing in this world: Anything that happens to me here, anything I experience or encounter or am about to experience.

That can take: Nothing that happens in my life can take something from me that will diminish me or my life experience in any way.

What is meant for you: Nothing in this life or my life circumstances can take away what is meant for me—what I'm meant to do, be, and experience here. I am on my path, and even if I can't see it right away, this is what is supposed to happen. Not necessarily to me, but *for* me.

I'm not sure why I took this message the way I did. Maybe it was because I had just finished crying, which had opened a space for something new. Maybe it was because I was experiencing loss and failure, wanting things to be different. In any case, the message was for me, and it supported me, as it touched those feelings of missing out on something, of missing Michael.

This all happened in an instant within me.

I looked up at the young woman. "Wow, that's beautiful. Thanks for the note."

When I started walking away, she said, "Have a great day."

I didn't get more than a few yards down the boardwalk before I had to turn around and talk with her about the envelopes. I found out she had just moved here from the Midwest. She supplemented her income by selling hand-sewn sweatshirts and surfboard covers made from old beach towels she picked up at Goodwill stores.

"What made you write the messages and put them in envelopes?" I asked.

"Oh, it's just something I do in the morning before I come down here," she said casually.

Even though I didn't have a use for surfboard covers or sweatshirts made from colorful towels, I bought one to give away as a gift. I thanked her again and wished her the best of luck.

Walking away, I was flooded with a feeling of acceptance, that I hadn't done anything wrong. *Everything I'm meant to experience, I am and will.* Nothing in this world could take that away. Once again, the tears came, but this time it was for a different reason: the sense that someone was watching out for me, that I was being taken care of, that I didn't have to do this on my own. Open and grateful, I continued slowly walking down the boardwalk.

***

As I reflected on this, I wondered what the chances were that I would receive a handwritten message while going through these emotions. I realized that part of me wanted a quick fix to make the pain go away. But another part of me recognized that what I really wanted was something more permanent that doesn't go away, that becomes part of me and who I am, that I take with me no matter what life brings.

CHAPTER TEN

WHY DIDN'T YOU TELL ME?

Saying hello is a powerful tool. When you say hello to something or someone, you set a direction for your awareness to move in. Therefore, whatever you say hello to greatly impacts your experience. If you say hello to chaos, to anger, to hurt, to division, to pain, then that's what you'll see. That's what you'll become more aware of. When you say hello to peace, to Spirit, to any aspect of wholeness, that's what you'll see and experience. The beauty of hello is that it's an invitation to experience something more. Hello is the beginning of a conversation. When you say hello to Spirit, you open up to everything. You can move in any direction, however fast or slow you'd like to go. Ultimately, you're saying hello to yourself. Recognize that the hello that goes outward is the same as the hello that goes inward.

***

When Michael passed, I very much wanted to connect with him, to know that he was okay. This isn't unusual for me. I'm often able to connect to people, living or dead, on a heart-istic level, which allows some communication to take place. It's a kind of direct sharing, as this communication doesn't always involve words. However, this time, I had a problem: the more I tried to connect with Michael, the more frustrated I got, and it just wasn't happening.

As I continued to attempt to communicate with Michael, I became more and more frustrated. I said to myself, *What the f*** is going on? I do this all the time, but now when I really want to communicate, I can't.*

The answer, a "downloaded message," came immediately: *Look at where you are. You are angry, frustrated, and stressed. Now look where Michael is. Shift where you are at. The communication is already there.*

These messages always show up in a way that I can understand, even if they make no sense to anyone else. When I received this message, it felt so obvious, the kind of advice someone would give to a person complaining they were tired and being told: "Well, why don't you sit down and rest?" I was so caught up in frustration and anger, trying to solve what I saw as a problem, that there was no room for me to hear anything else.

So I went inward, shifting where I was. I slowed down and relaxed, let go of trying to make something happen, and moved toward allowing the situation to unfold on its own. I slowly began to match the space where Michael was. With it came the knowing that this communication space already existed; I just had to open myself to it.

From there, I said hello and asked Michael what he wanted to show me in Spirit. He showed me an image of a young woman wearing a white dress that softly flowed over her shoulders and reached down to her feet. Her hair was black, and she wore a decorative headband with beads. She was very beautiful. This was his love. It let me know that he was not alone.

***

On the morning of Michael's passing, I had set an intention to allow the day to be filled with grace and ease. This really bothered me because that day didn't seem to match my intention at all. I asked God, "Where is the grace in this? Where's the ease?" As I asked these questions, I started feeling frustration that slowly turned to anger. Usually, I see things long before they arrive; I get a sense of what's coming down the road. So I yelled internally, "God, why didn't You show me?"

The answer came right away, loud and clear: "Because then you would have tried to stop it."

This time, I responded out loud, "Yeah, I would!"

I love how Spirit always meets us where we are, in the most beautiful and gentle and loving way, for us to hear.

Shortly after this, I was standing in Michael's bedroom when a feeling of Love completely enveloped his room, a sense that he was absolutely being taken care of. I was shown an image of Michael being embraced at home, a beautiful and loving embrace. It reminded me that his passing was at home; it wasn't violent, and it could have happened in so many other ways. More importantly, this showed me his passing wasn't random; it was about his journey. I needed to see and experience this directly for myself to begin shifting my own beliefs about what had happened.

Seeing something directly, within yourself, allows the experience and change to reach more deeply into the core of who you truly are. Instead of trying to bring in something from outside yourself to fill a void, direct seeing creates a space within yourself for something new to be born, something that will gradually work its way out into your life and dissolve the beliefs, thoughts, and feelings that do not serve you. It's an inner knowing beyond the mind that you don't have to control or put in energy to maintain.

While still in Michael's bedroom, I received a message about blessings:

When blessing someone and honoring them on their journey, see and honor their role in the divine plan and how it fits in and unfolds in the perfection of what is. When honoring their journey, that blessing, that relationship, will have no limit and no end, and the embrace will be felt in the whole Universe.

As I wrote down this message and took it in, I felt the connectedness of everything. I felt comforted somehow. I took a deep breath and then received the following message, a kind of instruction:

When grief comes, meet it with Love.

When sadness comes, embrace it with Love.

When beauty comes, meet it with Love.

When joy comes, be there with Love.

For in Love, All Things Are.

Love allows you to go anywhere, be anything. You asked Me about grace and ease during Michael's passing, and I showed you, that this was grace and ease when you saw how much more difficult it could have been—not only for you, but for Michael.

All your sufferings are the judgments and regrets you have in relationship to Michael. When he passed, all that got brought to the surface. They're what make loss so painful. The only thing that hurts is you hanging on to those ideas, judgments, and beliefs.

They are there for you to release, to allow yourself to be there with them, not to live in them...

My son shows me my regrets and expectations, especially where I need to love myself more deeply, where to honor myself and him more, and where to allow myself to be here more.

This is not easy when you're on a roller coaster of emotions. Just when you think you're done with an emotion or over something, something else triggers you, and you're off on another ride.

Chapter Eleven

Brother and Sister

Jen was close to Michael and had a difficult time seeing him struggle with drugs. As my daughter was just a year older than him, they did everything together growing up. They had a Jack and Jill bathroom, which is a shared bathroom, between their bedrooms. When they were young, I had to remove the bathroom doorknob so that they couldn't get into each other's bedroom after bedtime. Even after spending all day together, they would pass each other notes under the bathroom door, and I could hear them laughing and talking until late at night. When they were young, Michael's sister was usually the one directing, and Michael followed along. Later, those roles reversed.

Some siblings grow up physically together but are not very close. My son and daughter really did grow up together.

Their relationship stayed strong even into their teen years. They frequently ran to Target together to buy snacks. During high school, Jen started her own business photographing products for small businesses. She asked Michael if he would help model some of the products. At first, he said "Naw," but when offered ten bucks, he agreed.

They shared a bond of unspoken trust and love that was always there. It reminded me of the bond that I have with my own sister. It's not that we're in constant contact with each other, but there is a solid base, always there, that doesn't go away with time.

When things got tough, they relied on each other, especially when it came to situations that weren't so easy to talk about with a parent. They were each other's stable rock that didn't require maintenance, so Michael's passing was difficult for her.

***

Michael's Birthday

After nine months had passed, Michael's birthday was coming up. I didn't expect it to be hard, but it was emotional and brought back memories. I had the thought that we hadn't done all that much together, but after watching a few videos of Michael growing up, clearly we did. My wife said he'd had a good life.

A group of long-term friends sent over flowers with a signed card for Michael's birthday, which was really nice. They let us know they were still thinking about us and wanted to show their support.

A few days before Michael's birthday, we were contacted by the friend whom Michael had met the night before he passed. She knew Michael from high school, and he met up with her to help cheer her up and to just be there for her to talk to. We all met for brunch, and it was nice seeing her. We talked about her future and shared fun memories of Michael.

On the afternoon before Michael's birthday, someone knocked on the door. I thought it would be a salesman, but when I opened the door, I saw Michael's friend and his girlfriend. They brought over a small birthday cake and frozen mango mochi, which was one of Michael's favorite treats. They seemed to be doing well and just wanted to do something to remember Michael.

I was surprised that they came over. We had only met them maybe once or twice before. It showed me again how authentically his friends cared about him and the relationship that they had with him. As they were leaving, he shook my hand, and his girlfriend gave me a hug. I told them that I appreciated them stopping by. It meant a lot to me.

***

On what would have been Michael's twentieth birthday, Jen wrote a song called "No Cosmic Coincidences" and posted it on YouTube. Below are the lyrics and a link to the song.

https://www.youtube.com/watch?v=YOJnpG5b_vo

You should be older on your birthday
Yeah, it fuckin hurts me
That you're not here right now
I guess you'll always be nineteen
Even if the world keeps spinning round and round
Spinning round and round, round, round, round

So I'm screaming in my pillow
Wishing that I could know
Why the fuck did you have to leave
Now I'm looking for some signs
Waiting to align
Like that sticker and 999, 999, 999

I guess you'll never have a daughter
Wish I could of saw her
Growing up with you
So many milestones you're missing
And even if you're with me
I can't see you right now
I can't see you right now, now, now, now

There's a hole in my heart
There's a hole in my mind
And I'm so proud of you
I wish you had more time
Yeah, I don't believe in heaven
I don't believe in hell
But I do believe in something, and I hope you're doing well

I hope you are doing well, well, well, well

So I'm screaming in my pillow
Wishing that I could know
Why the fuck did you have to leave
Now I'm looking for some signs
Waiting to align
Like that sticker and 999
Like that sticker and 999, 999
I'll see ya soon

***

When I tuned into Michael, I could feel the love and joy surrounding the song that my daughter had written for his birthday. I love her honesty in that song and what it shows.

She also shared with me a vision she experienced, where she was looking at her dead body as all her family and friends felt grief and panic. In her vision, Michael was there beside her, and he told her, "This is the hardest part, seeing your family and loved ones go through sadness and grief."

CHAPTER TWELVE

SIGNS

Michael had been showing us signs of his presence, letting each of us know in different ways that he was there.

Some signs are subtle, and some are in your face. Signs are there to help you make connections, either with your loved ones or within yourself. Only you can decide what is a sign and what is not.

The interesting thing about signs is that they are specific to each person. The message and meaning of a sign are personal; the sign may not mean anything to an onlooker, yet it has a special meaning for us. Signs can come in all shapes, sizes, sounds, and even smells. If you're wondering if you've received a sign from your loved one, consider whether you keep noticing a recurring event. Don't dismiss it so quickly; stop and look at it. A sign may not always be obvious to you, and it may take some time to connect the dots and understand the meaning.

At first, you may have a hard time wrapping your mind around signs and wonder if you're just making up this stuff. But eventually, after so many experiences, signs become more difficult to deny.

The goal is not to make signs significant, but to make them ordinary and common. Communication should not be put on a pedestal, as anything you put on a pedestal can be brought down. What you know within yourself cannot be lost or taken. Instead of putting it on a pedestal, surround the sign with love and support. That can be as big or as narrow as it needs to be.

My daughter shared with me she can sometimes feel Michael's presence while driving in her car. He likes to say, "Hi," by pointing out all the cars that have a dog paw sticker. The sticker was an ongoing joke between them about, "Who saved who." Another sign for her is the number 999, a reference to a song by the rapper Juice WRLD. These are all signs for her, reminders that Michael is still here.

Funnily enough, while I was reviewing this section of the book, I received a sign from Michael. After Michael passed, I kept hearing a song in my head almost every day for about two weeks and I didn't understand why. It was a song by 38 Special about a breakup, about not wanting the relationship to be over, still being in love, second chances, and forgiveness. I wasn't sure why the song had stuck in my mind, but over time it faded.

I was in front of the computer, working on this chapter about signs, when the song popped into my head again. I stopped and pulled up the song online. I closed my eyes and followed the emotions within myself and the song, connecting and opening to more forgiveness.

When I opened my eyes and looked at the screen, the book had almost doubled in length. I took a closer look, scrolling through the manuscript to see what had happened. At the end of every chapter was a section of text I had considered adding. I laughed and shook my head. "Michael, you're making extra work for me." I smiled and embraced him even more, and, yes, I took this as a sign. Below is what was added:

It's early morning, I'm lying in bed, and I don't feel like getting up. Pulling the covers up over my head, I see a small blood stain in the shape of a tiny, perfectly formed heart. This causes me to burst out laughing. I recognize it's another way Michael is trying to reach out to me about love, about being loved. That I sometimes restrict how love is supposed to show up, the form it takes, and how I'm supposed to receive it. This heart reminds me to expand the space of connection, allowing love to reach me in more ways.

Take a look at how you receive love, where you may be restricting it, how narrow or wide your beliefs are around it. When you're ready, give yourself permission to open up in this area a little bit more. Embrace with warmth and compassion any parts within yourself that feel afraid, especially in regard to your loved ones.

CHAPTER THIRTEEN

DREAMS

My wife wanted to communicate with Michael as well. Shortly after Michael passed, she said to me, "Look, I don't have the same ability to communicate with Michael as you do, so anything that you get, I would like to hear."

My first thought was, "Yes, you do," but I didn't say that.

According to my wife, her guard is always up, and her mind is too busy, rational, and analytical to be able to receive anything. I told her that I was willing to share, but I wouldn't sugarcoat the truth for her. I would be honest about my experience. And she was okay with that. This request helped set the tone as we shared what we were experiencing and each grieved in our own ways.

I said, "If you want to communicate with Michael yourself, you need to ask. Ask directly for this and create a space to have it."

For my wife, this meant telling Michael to show up in her dreams.

She has a different style of communication than I do. Where I would ask or offer an invitation, she would demand. She normally communicated with Michael by being direct with a hint of humor, so this wasn't unusual for her.

A few days later, Michael came to her in a dream, just before she woke up.

Michael often came home late. My wife, an early riser, would already be up to let him in the front door. In her dream, Michael was knocking on the front door like he usually did, and my wife let him in and welcomed him home.

"Hi, Mom!" he said cheerfully, then gave her a big hug.

"I remember it well," my wife said. "I was half asleep and half awake, as if I were watching myself in the dream. It felt so real, I could feel the skin on his neck touch mine as we hugged."

This was Michael letting her know he was there.

***

Over the next few months, my wife shared the following three dreams with us.

Dream 1: "We were all walking on an iron bridge. I was looking down over the railing, and, next thing you know, Michael fell onto his back on the sandy ground below, which was maybe ten feet beneath the bridge. He didn't look injured, but he died from this fall. I felt like I was reliving the loss, feeling my grief all over again, yet I took this as another opportunity to process the loss by facing it head-on."

Dream 2: "It wasn't clear where we were, but he was stabbed in his stomach in front of me, and he died. Yet his face was peaceful, not at all traumatized. This was another opportunity to process my grief. I noticed the pattern that he seemed to die peacefully, and this was comforting."

Dream 3: "He was working in the garage when he looked to be around six years old. I went to him to say bye before going to work, and he looked up briefly, long enough to make eye contact, then cheerfully said, 'Bye, Mom!' and went back to his project. This was the moment it was clear to me that he wanted to say his goodbyes since he didn't get a chance to before he died."

"I treasure these dreams," my wife said. "He met me where I was, showing up for me in a way I could connect with him. He is still Michael, my carefree, easygoing, and fun-loving son."

***

My daughter also shared one of her dreams. Normally, her dreams don't have any sound, like a silent movie, so this dream with Michael had a big impact on her. In her dream, she walked into the kitchen, and Michael was there. He had on his blue robe with his back turned to her, making chocolate chip croissants. She heard the song "Trees" by Twenty One Pilots and interpreted that as Michael reaching out and saying hello. It was one of the clearest and most impactful signs she had gotten so far.

***

I wanted to know where Michael went after he passed, and not from a book or my personal belief system—I wanted to see for myself. I wanted to know he was okay. I had a few dreams that I wrote down right after having them, which helped. These were not what I would call ordinary dreams; they were somehow more vivid, and I was aware of myself in these dreams. Some might call it lucid dreaming, others might refer to it as a shamanic journey. Regardless of what you call it, these dreams showed me glimpses of what I wanted to know.

***

Michael was a free spirit. When he said hello to you, his smile said, "Everything is okay," and, "Let's have some fun." He wasn't threatening or combative, and that allowed him to interact with many different kinds of people with ease. It was part of the reason so many people liked him. At the same time, he didn't allow himself to be pushed around. Michael was definitely not afraid. I never saw him go looking for a fight, but he wouldn't back down when threatened. Michael wrestled, boxed, and joined a fight club to train in jujitsu.

I took him to his practices. One day in the car on the way back home, I asked Michael if he minded getting hit.

He said, "Naw. When I started doing this, I was worried about getting punched in the face, but after I got hit, I realized it wasn't so bad, and I lost my fear. So no big deal."

He had a unique balance of going with the flow and being tough at the same time. That freedom of spirit stayed with Michael throughout his life. No matter what was happening, I never saw that spirit be diminished.

While Michael was here physically, he struggled, fighting with a group of boys to the point where he carried a weapon to defend himself. For a parent, this was not an easy thing, as you want your kids to be safe. However, rule-setting, consequences, and lectures made no difference. Michael was strong-willed about certain things, and no one will hear what you have to say if they're not ready to receive it.

One day, I asked Michael what was going on. I thought he should try to avoid fights, have patience, and work out other solutions rather than engage in physical conflicts. I also know there is a time and place for everything.

When I asked Michael about this, he looked me straight in the eye and said, "Dad, these guys that are hassling me are not going to stop. It will make no difference talking with them. If they know I'm able to defend myself, they will leave me alone."

He shared some examples of this with me, and I knew he was being totally honest. Sometimes, no amount of thinking, "Can't we just get along?" works, and you need to be able to stand up for yourself.

In some ways, I feel a lot like Michael. People tend to see me as easygoing and laid-back, but when push comes to shove and I have to choose between fight or flight, I generally lean toward the fight side. I understood what he was saying, and I respected it.

***

I had a passing thought, wondering if Michael carried old unresolved struggles with him when he passed. After that, I had some dreams that helped answer this question.

In the dream, I was an observer, witnessing Michael in an open grassy space on a valley floor. (It was actually a large dark bird, but I knew it was Michael.) Up on a hill were what looked like six or seven large turkey vultures. Black with thorns and spikes protruding from their backs, they were looking for Michael or whatever trouble they could find. Without having spotted Michael yet, they moved down the hillside toward him. I watched, curious to see how he would handle this, whether he would fight or run away. As the vultures approached, Michael gently flew up the hill and landed on a branch high up in a tree. Looking up at him, I sensed he was totally calm and at peace. He wasn't the least bit concerned about the presence of the turkey vultures, and felt no need to fight or run. He didn't even care if they stayed or left. They had no power over him.

I was relieved that this struggle didn't continue with him after he passed. Seeing this helped me know within myself that he was at peace.

In the second dream, I was walking to meet Michael, but before I could see him, all these people, his students, met me. They excitedly told me how great Michael was and how he taught them so many things. Michael was their teacher and guide, and the students had a deep respect for him and honored his presence. I remember feeling out of place there, like I didn't know anything about how things worked.

This next part of the dream is more difficult to describe, but I saw that Michael was a "master teacher," a powerful guide, exactly where he was supposed to be on his journey. When I met Michael, he was excited and enthusiastic. His presence was vibrant. He showed me a bright, colorful wall of energy he was working with. It was the energy of new things he was creating there. It was alive and beautiful.

One thing I noted after waking from this dream was that Michael wasn't worried about us, or worried about anything for that matter. Maybe he had a knowing that we were already okay.

***

Michael also visited me in a dream on my birthday. I came into the house out of the garage and saw him sitting on the arm of the couch, facing the front door, with his gray hoodie on. I was so surprised and happy to see him. I ran over and hugged him, then pulled back to look into his eyes to make sure it was him. His eyes sparkled with a smile that only Michael could have. I knew it was him. My heart opened, and I smiled from the inside out.

We went on trips together, hiking some trails and kayaking. "Where have you been?" I asked. He didn't answer, so I moved the conversation to the here and now, telling him how happy I was to see him. As we were hiking, he moved faster than I did, so when there were forks in the trail, he scouted up ahead and showed me the way.

***

Each of us had dreams that spoke to us in a unique way, giving us messages or answering questions. After each dream, I felt closer to Michael, which helped me to resolve, on some level, the questions in my mind about where he was and if he was okay.

Chapter Fourteen

Bullets

I spend a lot of time at my home office desk, and even though it's covered in piles of paper, I know where things are. So when I found a black .50-caliber rubber bullet by my computer monitor one morning, I noticed.

At first, I thought Jen might have put the bullet there, so I asked her to come into my office. Holding the bullet in my hand, I asked, "Did you put this here? I found it on my desk."

"No, I don't know anything about that," she said. But she recognized it was a bullet that Michael used in his pistol, and her eyes welled up.

Michael enjoyed airsoft guns and had a pistol that shot .50-caliber rubber bullets, which are about the size of a small marble. He would go out with his friends or in our backyard to shoot.

"Maybe this is a sign from Michael letting you know he's still here," I said.

She smiled and gave me a big hug before she left.

I really didn't need more proof that Michael was here. But, in all honesty, I would take any sign that presented itself. Later, when I showed my wife the bullet, she didn't even know what it was.

At first, I thought I had forgotten about putting the bullet on my desk, but then other bullets started showing up. I found yellow BBs that he used in his airsoft gun on my office floor. I found others on small hills in the yard, which couldn't have rolled down from somewhere.

One morning, I walked into my office with socks on and stepped on a yellow BB in the doorway. I picked it up to examine it more closely, asking myself, *Okay, what's going on here? What's the meaning of this?*

As I waited, the answer came: *Oh, it's not so much about the meaning of this yellow BB. It's because of something you are wanting.*

This caused me to redirect my focus inward. I stopped trying to figure out the message behind the bullets and instead looked at what was it I wanted.

Upon reflection, what I wanted was a closer relationship with Michael, for our relationship to be open and free. What came to my awareness right behind that reflection was that, in order to have a deeper relationship, I needed to forgive and let go of my judgments. I had a lot of work to do: forgiving myself for things I did and did not do, and forgiving Michael for things he did and did not do.

Those bullets keep showing up, enough times now that my mind can no longer dismiss them with a logical explanation. They helped my mind break out of the box of what is possible and bring validation, a visceral feeling that Michael is still here in ways that I can't explain and are difficult to ignore. Now, when I find another bullet and mention it to my wife and daughter, we all just laugh and say, "Hi, Michael."

***

Trash into Treasures

Sitting in the backyard one day, I see the yellow BBs Michael used to shoot from his pellet gun. I smile, remembering how I used to see these BBs as trash—these plastic bullets that never go away, never dissolve, that just get into the pool and clog up the filter. But now they represent good memories of him having fun shooting in the backyard. It's funny how trash can turn into treasures.

Other people have also shared with us that Michael has visited them to let them know he's here. In a way, we're all learning a new form of communication with Michael. It's continually evolving, and it's just as real, only in a different way. The more I release my judgments of myself and Michael, the deeper and closer I can be to him.

CHAPTER FIFTEEN

CONNECTION

I wrote down the following downloaded message as I received it:

Jeff, you talk to yourself about how you want a deeper connection with Michael, but look at the connection you have. Look at what you are doing. Look at what you are writing. People don't write books, pray, or offer blessings to people they don't have a strong connection with. You have the idea that it could be or should be something different. It is already so strong you can feel the power of it, in those rushes of emotion and will and energy that flow through you even as you are writing this now; it is so powerful.

Instead of trying to make it deeper, trying to make it more, rest. Rest in the relationship that you have. The one that is already there. See those memories and images and know that it is already there for you, full and complete. Let go of the idea that something is lacking. Trying to fill a hole never works in these situations. Remember, you put the meaning around things and events. It can be a strength and also a curse, depending on what you choose. Remember, your connection is strong; it is based on you. Your heart has nothing to be ashamed of. If you want something to be different, explore what is already here, what is already part of you. You will find that the difference you are looking for has been there all along. Relax and allow love to fill in any and all spaces.

There's a pause in the message, and then it continues:

Do you know how lucky you are? All the direct signs from Michael, all the messages, the physical objects appearing, synchronicities—not everyone has those opportunities. I know you take that for granted, as you've had that all your life. Validate and acknowledge, with Michael, that line of communication. This communication is not a one-off but is there all the time. Wherever there is love, it is a channel for communication, a space of sharing. Honor where you are. Where you are in your heart. That space is so powerful and without limits.

This message reminded me to change the focus from what I want to what I already have, and not try to be somewhere I'm not. When you go within and look at the connection you have with your loved one, it can sometimes be overshadowed by judgments, grief, and other emotions. Of course your relationship with them has changed, but their essence and your heart connection with them is still alive and available to you.

One of these connection points can be with your inner child. It's the part of you that is fun, free, spontaneous, and filled with laughter. Especially if your loved one has a silly, fun-loving side to them, connecting with them on this level lets love flow freely. This is different from communicating with them as a parent. Yes, parents love their children, but they also worry and carry expectations and disappointments. Connecting with your loved one from your inner child to their inner child can broaden and deepen your relationship, allowing you to be together on a new level.

Communicating with someone who's not physically here isn't so different from talking with friends and relatives who live far away. I still have a relationship with them inside me, even if I don't often see them physically. It's the same with Michael. He's not physically here, but I have a continuing and living relationship with him.

Some might think this is just a form of denial that someone has passed. The difference, I would say, is that one of these viewpoints has me looking to past memories, longing for the past, while the other viewpoint lives in the present moment, moving and growing from there. For me, relationships don't just involve experiencing what happens externally; more importantly, they include what happens internally. This kind of relationship is not a one-way street, where you're just talking to yourself in your head or putting things out into the ether. This two-way communication happens within yourself, in a heart space of freedom where possibilities are. It has always been there. In this space, most of the external chatter isn't there to distract you, and you can take your relationship to another level. In some ways, it can be more fulfilling—not in the sense of doing and remembering things, although that can be there, too, but in how you share time with each other.

Relationships nurtured and loved in this heart space never die. Having this relationship with Michael allows me to process grief in a way that is authentic for me; it has allowed the healing process to not be forced or a "fake-it-till-you-make-it" situation.

This relationship that I'm speaking of, that I'm pointing toward, has so much to offer. It can deepen in every area, and move in whatever direction you feel. It includes everything, all your thoughts and feelings. It can be honest, real, raw, tender, and beautiful if you don't turn away.

***

What Remains

I'm discovering that, as time goes on, my relationships with Michael and others are deepening. When I set aside the distractions of everyday life, what is left are the connections I feel. My connection with Michael grows and changes as if he were here physically. It expands my beliefs about what a relationship is, about who I am. This happens because of what remains.

So, what remains after someone passes? Some might say you have your memories, and, yes, those can be beautiful, wonderful, and sometimes painful. But what is also left is my connection with Michael, how I feel, how I can be with him now. When you spend a lot of time in your heart with someone, the relationship grows and deepens. Whether they are there physically or not, the connection is not a static thing you simply revisit. It's alive and, when nurtured, can grow.

This deepening carries over to the people around me: my wife and daughter, my dad and sister, my friends. There is more appreciation, a kinder and gentler acceptance of who they are on their own journey with life. I feel blessed and grateful for this gift.

I still have that desire to speak with Michael, to communicate with him, to find out how he's doing: Is he okay? Where is he? What is he doing? Those are things I'm interested in seeing for myself. This might seem to be impossible at first glance, but the power behind this desire is huge for me. It's more than a connection between a father and son.

I don't claim to know what happens after we die or how it works; all I can share are my glimpses of what I see and experience.

CHAPTER SIXTEEN

MICHAEL'S LETTER

It's difficult to watch someone struggle. There's a feeling of helplessness, especially as a parent, when drugs and addiction are involved—wanting to help, feeling your way through the choices of when to step in and when to back off, yet not really knowing how to. Drugs can slowly change from an experience of trying new things and experimenting, to something that begins to take over. You can see the person you know and love changing before your eyes. As a parent, you hold your breath, knowing that things could take a turn for the worse on any given day. At the same time, you show them a positive path that they must choose for themselves. It affects everyone in the family. Michael was a strong person, not easily swayed by others, who was finding his path and having fun with his friends. Michael walked that fine line.

***

A few months after Michael passed, I went outside to check the mailbox and found a letter. I was confused by what I saw: a letter addressed to

Michael written in pencil. The return address, also in pencil, showed Michael's name and address.

What is this? I wonder. *Is this some kind of joke? Is somebody just messing with us?*

I brought the letter inside and called my wife and daughter into the kitchen. We gathered round and opened it up, shocked to find that Michael himself had hand written the letter. We opened it and started reading:

A Letter to My Future Self

"Hello, this is Michael from the past prior to graduation. How has it been going in the workforce? How does it feel to have your own source of income you earned with your own work? I have a feeling I will be doing productive things toward my future by then. I also assume you and Denice are still going strong, and I am happy for you.

I want you to continue to improve yourself, even if you are happy with what you have accomplished. Make sure you remember to take up a hobby and occupy your time with things you like doing. Always remember to keep moving forward and have a goal in mind to stay motivated. I hope you find something to sink endless hours into. And just know that I am proud of you."

We could only guess that it was part of a high school project, mailed by the school at a later date. Reading this letter was very emotional for us. It felt like he was right there, sharing with us. Seeing him talk to himself in this way at the age of eighteen showed me again the positive inner strength he had. Michael was consistent in his personality and outlook on life, and his letter reflected this. I would hear these qualities over and over again as other people and his friends talked about him.

***

Sigil

I was working from my home office one day when Jen came in and said, "Dad, I'm going to get a tattoo for Michael. Do you know what a sigil is?"

"No, what's that?" I asked.

"Here, let me show you. I'm using the last line in Michael's letter. See, it starts like this..."

She got out a piece of paper and wrote "I am proud of you."

"Then you cross off all the vowels. And you're left with..."

She scratched out all the vowels on the paper, leaving only m, p, r, d, f, and y.

"Then you take those letters and combine them to make a symbol. I'm going to use Michael's handwriting. I don't want any written words in the tattoo, but I'll know what this symbol means."

"Oh, I see," I said. "That's pretty cool. When are you going to do that?"

"Sometime next week," she said.

Below is the sigil symbol she created and her tattoo:

The dagger tattoo is a reminder of a time when she went with Michael to a sketchy part of town. Michael was picking up drugs and didn't want her going inside with him, so he left a dagger with her in the car in case things went sideways. Michael told me once that those guys all carried guns. This didn't happen often, but it gives you a sense of the people he was involved with.

The matchstick is the first stick-and-poke tattoo my daughter gave herself, which is a traditional style of tattooing with a stick and a needle that Michael also used to tattoo himself.

Chapter Seventeen

A No Becomes a Yes

Sometimes in life, you end up doing things you never thought you would do, or find yourself in situations you never thought you'd be in. Life has a way of bringing you to the point where you have to take another look at what you believe to see if those things still make sense and are still true for you.

For me, tattoos had a negative connotation, like you couldn't get a certain type of job if you had one. Otherwise, I hadn't given tattoos a lot of thought; they just didn't appeal to me.

For Michael, tattoos meant something different. They were a way for him to memorialize certain events that were meaningful to him. He didn't get them because he thought they looked good or to impress people, but to represent memories or lessons that had made an impact on him. One of the places Michael worked let each employee put their favorite saying under their name on their name tag. Michael's tag said, "I love tattoos."

Michael had given himself several tattoos. He used a stick-and-poke method, which involves a needle dipped in ink attached to a stick. I didn't like tattoos, but for anyone who has ever tried to stop their teenager from doing something that they're passionate about, well, good luck with that. He had the symbol 999 on his arm, representing a song by the rapper Juice WRLD. The rap star said that the number was an inversion of 666, which is known as the mark of the beast. He added, "999 represents taking whatever ill, whatever bad situation, whatever struggle you're going through and turning it into something positive to push yourself forward." This is something that Michael also did in his l ife.

***

One evening in the living room, Michael and I were having a conversation about life. We had just watched a YouTube video that asked whether life was predetermined or if we had the freedom to choose. All the details escape me now, but what I remember about that conversation is the mutual respect we had for each other's points of view. As the conversation wound down, I said to Michael, "I'm glad you're here." That was my way of telling Michael I loved him.

"I'm glad you're here, too," he said.

Michael went into the bathroom, and after he came out he asked if I wanted to get a tattoo with him. I was a little surprised. I told him I appreciated that, but it wasn't my thing.

He asked, "Is it because of the pain of getting it?"

"No," I said. "That doesn't bother me. It's just not my thing"

He smiled and said, "Okay."

When I told my wife the next day that Michael had asked about getting a tattoo together, she asked, "What did you say?"

"I said no."

"You know, Michael won't ask again," she said.

"Yeah, I know."

Michael lived in the moment. One moment, something would feel right, and then in the next, it wouldn't. Michael was the type of person who hardly ever asked for things. In that way, he was very independent. Making a connection was important to me, so I didn't want to just let this pass. I tried to think of an alternative.

I brought up the idea to him the next day that maybe, instead of getting tattoos, we could make our own gratitude symbols out of the same piece of wood to represent our connection. He said okay. We made gratitude symbols carved in oak and carved our names on the back, then cut the wood into two pieces so that we could each have half. It was good, but I could tell that for him it wasn't quite the same. I got the sense that he was just going along with it because it was what I wanted rather than what he wanted. It wasn't the same as getting a tattoo on his body.

Gratitude Symbols

A few months earlier, my daughter handed me a yellow sticky note and asked me to draw a small heart on it. She said she wanted to get a tattoo for her birthday with all our hearts on it, so my wife, Michael, and I all drew small hearts for her. I had to make several attempts to finally draw one that didn't look like it was done by a two year old.

A few days after Michael passed, Jen said she was going to get a tattoo on her finger of the heart Michael had drawn. She asked my wife and me if we wanted to get tattoos on our fingers as well. When she asked me, the old negative feelings about tattoos began surfacing within me. But this time, I paused. I stopped the mental chatter, turned my attention inward, and asked myself if I wanted to get a tattoo. As I brought my attention to the tattoo, the space felt open. It felt like an open space of honoring Michael, like connecting with family. It felt right.

I turned to my daughter and said, "Well, it looks like I'm getting a tattoo."

Jen made the appointment. She had been to this tattoo artist before and liked her work. As we were getting ready to go and heading out to the car, there was a sense of excitement and nervousness. My daughter put on some numbing cream and asked my wife and me if we wanted some.

My wife said, "No, I want to feel everything." In fact, she had decided to not only get the heart tattoo but also Michael's name on her arm.

I said, "Sure, why not?"

I was told that fingers are sensitive because there's not a lot of flesh there, so you can feel it more when the tattoo is being done. Before I put the cream on, I asked Jen if this stuff stunk. She just looked at me and smiled without saying anything. I rubbed some of the cream on my finger, but it didn't smell.

The tattoo place looked like it used to be a single-family home. Inside was a big open room with artwork and tattoo designs hanging on the walls. The bookshelves were stocked with various items for sale, postcards, and small animal skulls. Other people were getting tattoos as the sound of buzzing needles filled the air. We sat down on the couch in the waiting area, and our tattoo artist came around to greet us. She was young, maybe in her mid-twenties, and had a lot of tattoos. Come to find out, she did a lot of them herself. Her earlobes were stretched to hold elongated earpieces. It reminded me of pictures I had seen in

National Geographic of the tribespeople who stretched their earlobes to large proportions.

As she approached, she smiled and welcomed us. I immediately liked her. Her eyes were bright, and I got the sense that she was a good person. This put me right at ease as Jen handed her the paper with the heart that Michael drew. She copied it into her iPad to begin making the template.

My wife wanted to go first, so Jen and I waited our turn. When it was my turn, I moved toward the back of the room and sat in a well-worn, slightly tilted chair. The tattoo artist said my finger had a little more space to work with, so if I wanted to get the heart a little larger, I could.

"No," I said. "I want to have the same heart as my wife and daughter."

I leaned back, and she began.

It turned out that the numbing cream Jen and I used was way past its expiration date and had lost its potency, but it didn't matter. We all got tattoos on our fingers, and then the artist covered them in the after-care wrap, what's called a "second skin," to help prevent infections. I looked at my tattoo and liked it. It felt like a match for me; it was a representation of something permanent.

We talked about our experience and what it was like. My wife said she felt like someone was cutting her arm and that she wanted it to be like that. Maybe for her, it represented not only Michael's memory but also the pain that was there.

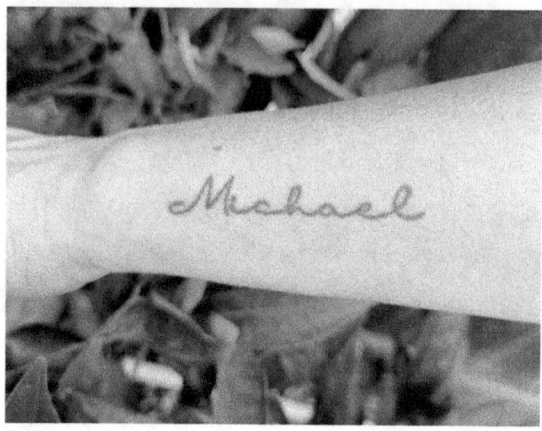

I think that Michael would've laughed, in his fun way of saying, "See? You and everyone ended up getting a tattoo." I miss that laugh and smile.

***

Two days after Michael passed, Jen won a giveaway for a custom illustration by artist Jennifer Corra of Crescent Moon Archives. Jen saw this as a sign from Michael, letting her know he was still there. Below is the artwork, including our matching heart tattoos.

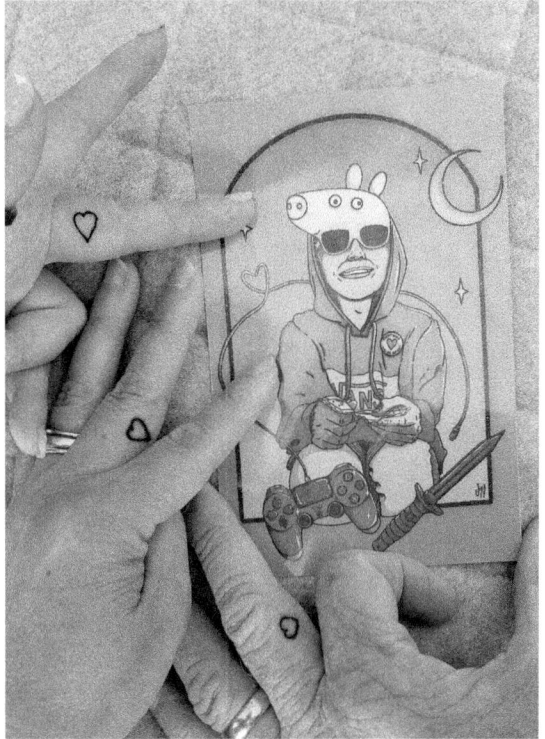

Heart Tattoos

Along the way, opportunities will arise for you to honor your loved one. Some people may offer you suggestions on how to do this, but what's important is that it comes from you. It may have a serious tone, or it can be something fun and silly. When looking for ways to honor and connect with your loved one, it's helpful to say hello to your own heart first, to get in touch with your inner self, and then say hello to them. See the connection you already have and the beauty of the times you shared. Stop for a moment and notice how your loved one may be reaching out to you. Pay attention to what shows up and feels right. It's often the simplest thing that offers the deepest connection.

Chapter Eighteen

Time

When my son and daughter were young, I encouraged them to make decisions by asking themselves questions and seeing what answer they received, rather than always asking someone else. I do this for myself all the time. I don't always get the right answer, but I'm more in touch with myself, making it easier to correct my course as things unfold.

When I try to solve things with just my mind, I often second-guess myself or play the "what if" game. When the answers come from within, from my intuition, I experience them directly and they are complete the moment I receive them. They're not always what I expect, but if I give them enough space to be heard, they show up in a graceful way.

***

Several months before Michael passed, I was mad at him. It was 2:00 a.m., and he wasn't home. No phone call, he wasn't answering his phone, nobody seemed to know where he was, and I was getting worried. When he finally walked in the door, I was still up, waiting on the couch. He didn't want to talk and went directly into his room, which wasn't okay for me.

"We'll talk later," I said.

The next morning, I was still angry, thinking, *Hey, at least a phone call, a little common courtesy. Show a little respect.*

As I waited for Michael to wake up, I thought about what I wanted to tell him regarding doing the right thing, asking permission, and being responsible. I knew it would probably be deflected, but I wanted to say it anyway.

Then I stopped to check in with myself. I asked, *What's the best course of action here? What needs to happen that will be best for me and also Michael?*

My intuition came in loud and clear: *Give Michael the handmade wooden plaque.*

Wait, what?!

This intuitive message was pretty much the opposite of what I was feeling; I wanted to talk about responsibility. I took a moment to pause before I agreed. The oak plaque I'd been working on had the word "Time" on it, and some waves carved into it. For me, it represented the changing nature of time, how it's not set when we move through it, and we only have so much of it.

When Michael woke up, he came down and sat at the dining room table. His hair was matted, and his eyes were barely open.

"I want to give you something," I said.

"What?"

I handed him the plaque. "Here, this is for you, Michael. It's something I made."

On the back, it said "To Michael, From Dad." I shared with him the meaning it had for me, and his whole demeanor changed. When our eyes met, he relaxed.

"Thanks, Dad."

Maybe what he needed was more time and a little more support for what was going on in his life. The lecture wasn't so important when I looked back on it; that was more about me trying to feel better. Sometimes a lecture isn't as important as just being there. Sometimes connecting with someone is more helpful than correcting them.

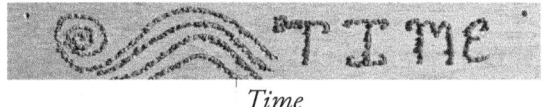

Time

CHAPTER NINETEEN

VIEW ROCK

No matter how much you do as a parent, you cannot save your children from pain. Of course, you don't want to see your children suffer, but you cannot protect them from everything, especially their own choices. They're on their own journey, and no matter what it may seem like, you are not in control. The question becomes, how can you love and support them to make the best choices for themselves and to move into becoming more of who they truly are?

***

I continued to struggle with the feeling of failing Michael. This feeling of responsibility around his passing weighed heavily on me, and the overwhelming thoughts that I could have done more were punishing me. This is something that can continually run around in your head with seemingly no solution. You can get stuck there for a long time if you let yourself. I was deeply conflicted, searching for a way to reconcile this within myself.

***

The hike up to View Rock takes a little effort, but the view overlooking the valley and the small mountains makes it worth it.

View Rock is a place I sometimes go to unplug, clear my head, and have some time for myself. The large granite boulders on the hillside are the perfect place to sit while overlooking the valley floor. No one is around. You can watch the circling hawks float effortlessly on the breeze, looking for their next meal. It feels spacious there, and time doesn't feel as important. You can see for miles. It's beautiful.

Up at View Rock one morning the emotional heaviness had once again returned. Sitting on a boulder, feeling a gentle breeze and the warm sun on my face, I looked out over the valley. Then I took a deep breath, closed my eyes, and started a conversation with the Universe. I was open, raw, and honest as I moved into this inner space and asked questions about feeling like a failure: *What is this? What's this all about? What is my responsibility in all of this? What am I responsible for? What is my responsibility to Michael, and what's my responsibility to other people?*

I've discovered that if I am totally raw and honest about what I ask, with no expectations, then what shows up is equally raw and honest.

I felt a warm embrace begin to soothe my stressed-out body. My mind fell away as I was taken to another place. Connecting more fully with my emotions, I moved more deeply into my inner self—the one that has infinite knowledge. I went deeper inward until I was shown a chamber. I saw Michael on his life's journey—not just the life he'd had here, but also his soul's journey. How he was on his path with his experiences and his choices. I recognized that this journey was between him, his true self, and God, and this journey was honored. It showed me that everything was and is as it's supposed to be. Nothing needed to be fixed. Witnessing this directly, I felt no doubt, no questioning-mind chatter. I was right there, experiencing it for myself. In that same instant, I also saw that my self-judgment was the failure, that I was trying to take over, to control Michael's journey and experiences—trying to "save him." No matter how well-intentioned that may be, I saw how starkly silly it was.

Who was I to think that I was in a position to do that, to take over the Universe's job? Let alone the fact that I couldn't even know what the Universe's job was. That struck me as so silly, so funny, so ridiculous in the moment, that I actually laughed out loud. That laugh took me out of that introspective space, and I opened my eyes to see if anybody else was around me. No one was. As I looked out over the valley with tears streaming, my heart opened, and something dark and heavy was released in that moment. I could breathe a little more easily. There was a lightness within me.

Walking back home, I reflected on what I had just experienced. It reminded me of a small child who was trying their best to accomplish something while the parent watched over them, knowing that it wouldn't work yet lovingly smiling, staying with them, knowing they are safe, beautiful, and loved.

This experience created the space to begin a true healing process toward not feeling responsible for Michael's death. This is not something that you can just tell yourself or try to convince your mind of; it has to come from a deeper place within you for it to have a base, a true place to live.

Once in a while, those thoughts and judgments about being a failure still pop up, but when they do, I know in my heart they aren't true. They no longer have the same power over me, and I don't try to fight them or get rid of them.

Instead, when they come, I try to offer myself a little more compassion for the one who feels that way. Those thoughts continue to fade as I don't feed them, and I'm grateful for that.

Ultimately, you can't fail at something you're not in charge of, and beating yourself up does nothing to honor the person who has passed.

***

I was sitting on the couch a few days after visiting View Rock when the thought of needing to help Michael with his struggles came up again. This time, I decided to ask Michael directly about what I was feeling. I wrote down what he shared as it came through:

You are trying to save me from pain and suffering. But those things are not for you to face, not for you to solve. Those are things that I'm looking at, that I'm working on to help grow to become more of who I am. Your job is not to take away that pain. Your job is not to take away those experiences or to shield me, but to honor what is. You cannot take responsibility for those things and punish yourself and see yourself as failing, for you have not failed. There is no way you can fail. Your suffering, your hurt, is trying to take responsibility for those things which you are not responsible for. It's not your job, it's not your duty, it's not your obligation.

Moving outside of what is yours, what it is you are here to do, is a kind of suffering. You are moving and doing things here, becoming more you, being here, being you here. That is your job here. You do that by loving yourself, honoring yourself in the things that you are looking at, that you are sharing, that you are growing, for all these things are interconnected and are one growth, one being—your growth you are sharing. You are growing for all. Your growth is a benefit for all.

You do not know this completely. You have a small idea of what this means, but you have no idea how big of an impact you are making when you choose love, when you choose to love yourself, when you choose to be here and honor and bless yourself and others. You have no idea. You are right when you see that it's not about sitting and being with grief and accepting grief, accepting sadness—it's about being with the one who is experiencing grief, honoring the one who is feeling sadness, being with that person, being with you, loving you, honoring you.

Continue being compassionate with yourself, patient, understanding. We love you and honor you. You are doing so well.

I'm not sure why I heard, "We love you," but that's how it came through.

What I got from this was how important it is not to try to magically accept your grief and sadness, but to be with the one who is grieving. To focus and be active with the part of me who is experiencing these feelings. To give to myself, my grieving self, acceptance and compassion.

Hearing this was helpful for me, especially the part about not just working on acceptance of sadness and grief, some artificial standard I was supposed to meet.

CHAPTER TWENTY

THROWING BULLETS

The sewer, as I call it, is a private place, a connection of underground tunnels and rooms made for storm drainage. The sewer doesn't sound like such a great place; it's not a place I would want to hang out, and my daughter calls it gross. But for Michael, the sewer offered another space for him to have fun with his friends. He didn't seem to mind the smells, water, darkness, or little critters that lived there. He liked this place, and it was a part of his life. It was also a good spot to test out some of his projects in a "safer" location.

***

Michael invited me to go with him to the sewer once to show me what a flare gun looks like when it's fired off in a pitch-black tunnel. Any of you who have been in complete darkness know that your eyes naturally continue to look for light. I plugged my ears, and as my eyes were still searching for the light, Michael fired off the flare gun. The bang echoed off the walls, and a brilliant red ring of light formed as it moved down the tunnel. It was amazing. I felt as if I were in a science fiction movie where one ship had just fired upon another. Michael's enthusiasm was contagious, and he loved sharing what he was excited about. I must admit: It looked pretty cool.

***

Shortly after Michael's passing, Jen's boyfriend was at our house, when he said he was going to the sewer to have a ceremony for Michael. He asked us if we wanted to go, and we said, "Sure." I was surprised that he was doing this. I didn't realize he felt such a connection with Michael. When my daughter's boyfriend would come over to the house, Michael would be excited to show him his newest knife or talk about possible strategies to defeat the bosses in the *Dark Souls* video game.

He had a tray of things for the ceremony: candles, a bee, a knife, a lighter, flowers, and a dead bird. My wife brought A.1. steak sauce and hot Takis chips, as those were Michael's favorites. Jen brought earbuds since Michael was always losing his, and I brought empty rifle shells to represent some of the projects he worked on.

The four of us hopped in the car for the short drive. This was my wife's first time going to the sewer. I wondered how she would feel about this place, but she didn't seem to mind. We parked and took a short walk through a forested area, past the "no trespassing" signs, and down a small hill of loose dirt. Bits of trash were strewn about, and we were careful where we stepped. This wasn't a place where you wanted to slip. We made our way along the edge of overgrown plants, passed a small pool of water with water spiders and crayfish scurrying about, and then finally arrived at the main entrance.

The large opening reminded me of a cave entrance. You can walk right in, but you can only see a little way down the tunnel, as it soon gets swallowed up by darkness. Water runs down the middle, but it isn't very deep. These tunnels go for miles underground, sometimes with short drop-offs and built-in ladders that go to other levels, and sometimes opening into large rooms. There's evidence of other people having been there.

We turned our flashlights on and began to make our way farther into the tunnel. Eventually, we found a spot to put the tray down, light the candles, and form a circle. We said our goodbyes in a tribute to Michael, each in our own way. At the end, we each took an empty shell and threw it down the dark tunnel. It felt good doing this, a way to share, honor, and respect the experiences Michael had had in this place and the fun he'd had while he was here. We left most of the items he liked down there and headed back to the car.

Most people wouldn't picture the sewer as a place for a ceremony, but for Michael it was perfect.

Chapter Twenty-One

Celebration of Life

Everyone pursues what they think they want. We take actions believing it will lead us to the best results, but we're not always successful. We interpret our experiences and assign them meaning to match what we are trying to achieve. Each person we meet along the way gives us something. Sometimes we ask them for things they cannot give, which can be disappointing, but each person can only give who they are, and they can only give from where they are now on their journey. We cannot expect anything else.

Each of us learns in our own personal and unique way. No one has had the same experiences as you, and in that way you're one of a kind. To honor each other means we recognize each person's journey. We especially need to recognize our own journey, that we are where we are, meeting each experience in the best way we know how.

If we're very lucky, we find people who genuinely care about us, who transcend the ups and downs of life, and who we genuinely care for as well. All things are possible in this love, and it allows us to thrive and grow. So honor yourself and allow that love to be with you. You are on your own journey. Offer it when you can and share it with others. For, in the end, nothing else really matters. I believe Michael shared those parts of himself with others, and that's why he had such a lasting impact on so many lives.

***

One thing I learned from Michael's friends after he passed was that he was the same person with them as he was at home. Of course, he was a little freer and crazier with his friends, but the things his friends said he talked about with them were the same things he talked about with us. This gave me a sense of comfort, knowing that at least on some level he could be himself no matter where he was. I kept hearing from others that Michael was the most genuine person they knew, authentic and easygoing yet not easily swayed by other people. If he believed he was right, he wouldn't back down. He would tell you if he honestly thought what you were doing was stupid, but he wouldn't try to convince you to change your mind.

***

The celebration of life was difficult to put together because our family is spread out. Some of us are in Japan, some are in the Midwest, and others are on the East Coast. Since Covid-19 made it difficult to travel, we decided to do a virtual ceremony over Zoom. (Zoom, for those of you who may not know, is a web-based meeting space where you can have many people join in at the same time to see and hear each other.)

I wanted to honor Michael and his life, and I tried to include everyone I could in pictures and short video clips. My wife even hired a Japanese interpreter, which allowed her family to participate in the Zoom meeting as well. I was so glad she did. But going through the pictures and videos of Michael was tough. I couldn't do it for long without getting so emotional that I couldn't continue. Doing this, though, helped me see the bigger picture of Michael's journey, reminding me that his life is not defined by one event—that there's more, a lot more.

Throughout the ceremony, we highlighted Michael's experiences, his trips with friends, and some of our funny stories.

At the end of the celebration of life, we opened up the meeting to anyone who would like to share something. I think hosting the meeting online helped in this situation. No one had to get dressed up or stand in front of a group of people. Here, people could participate as they were. Some people were at home, some people were in their car—it didn't really matter.

Earlier, I wondered if people would feel free to share in this way. Who would be there? What would they say? I was totally surprised. I had no idea that so many people would come forward to honor Michael, to share how he influenced their lives and how important he was to them. I saw the value of the connections that were there. Below are snippets of a few stories that were shared:

***

Michael was the one who kept me grounded. Just lots of crazy stuff, always a blast. Michael always lived in the moment, you know I always appreciated that. He always appreciated the people and things he had in his life. He didn't dwell on crappy things, always a good time together. One of the smartest, wisest, most inventive and creative people I know. Above all, he was a natural leader; he had this ability to gather everybody together and get everyone on the same wavelength, on the same page. Michael would include all of his friends, which was a little weird in this group. An unbreakable bond. We could just come together and talk about things and completely open up on a spiritual level. He was just somebody that you could always open up to. Even if you didn't have those same feelings, he would connect with you. We did the same for him; it was always like no filter.

***

Going out on the hiking trails at night, I would be really tired, but Michael would want to just keep going. He had a lot of energy. No matter how much time passed between the last time we saw each other, he would speak to me as if no time had passed. Grateful that he had his influence on me; no one like him.

***

Sixth grade, I talked with Michael on the first day of school and told him about my uncle's death. He said something like, "Death is a part of life," and I really believed him when he said it. He was one of the most emotionally intelligent people I've ever talked to. He really helped me.

***

He sourced his wisdom from who he was. He didn't compromise on that. He was mischief without malice. He was very excited about his knives, and he had to show you what he was excited about. There was a purity in that. I miss him.

***

At a birthday party, we were playing this game where you had to bite something that was hanging from a string, and I was worried about losing a tooth. Michael said to me, "You got to lose them eventually."

***

He was a phenomenal person. He was always so willing to give parts of himself to everyone he'd meet.

***

Michael doing silly things, making a suit out of a watermelon at the park. I'm so happy I met him. He always stayed true to himself. He never really changed; that's what I really liked about him. He left with no regrets, that's for sure. I'll miss him a lot. He gave me so many memories.

***

I don't think I've ever met someone else who I can be 100% certain they were 100% genuinely good at heart. I think Michael was that one person for me, who I could set as a standard for what a good friend was. Thank you, Michael. I miss you.

***

I was blown away by these testimonies. It was incredibly powerful for me to hear about Michael's connections with his friends. I mean, I knew they were tight, but I didn't realize how much so until I heard it from them.

I began seeing my relationship with Michael in a new way. I looked at my roles: being a parent, helping him grow, and learning how to love someone without knowing how to do it. As I reflected on this, I saw the bigger picture of my own life: how valuable it is, how wonderful, how painful, how confusing, how beautiful. I realized that the things that life brings with it are rich and to be appreciated, even the not-so-nice parts.

This broadened view helped me see my place in the world: how I fit in, how I am part of that journey as well. Through Michael's journey, I recognized that, in some way, we are all on the same path with the same center. It's not easy, but when I let this recognition in, I feel more connected and expanded—and in a strange way, taken care of.

I don't claim to know where all this leads, but in that connection, I know we are not alone on our journey.

Letting Go

Chapter Twenty-Two

Last Wishes

One thing about death is that it doesn't feel like there is a choice about it or the changes it brings. I don't consciously choose the changes that happen, which is very different than when I decide to change some aspect of my life. It's as if death has a will of its own, its own agenda. Maybe that's why the inner transformations that happens in relation to death feels uncontrolled, random, chaotic, and sometimes harsh.

***

My wife, who works as a social worker in the cancer and radiation department at a hospital, sees a lot of people who are faced with difficult situations. I'm not sure I could do her job, but I know she helps a lot of people. Part of her job involves having people fill out forms for healthcare directives, which cover topics like end-of-life circumstances, burial, and who decides what happens if someone is unable to make decisions for themselves. These are topics most people prefer to avoid.

About eight months before Michael passed, my wife told us we needed to fill out these forms. My eighteen-year-old son and nineteen-year-old daughter weren't too enthusiastic about this. Who thinks about that stuff when you're that age? I didn't really want to do it either, but I went along with it. My wife can be insistent, and we all knew she wasn't going to let this one go, so we all filled out the forms.

After we finished, we sat around the dining room table and read each other's wishes. It was an eye-opening experience, and I'm glad we did it. Michael, of course, had this carefree attitude that things would work out. So in his lighthearted way, with a grin on his face, he said that at the end of his life, he wanted to be cremated and blasted off in some fireworks. He thought that would be fun.

Oh, wow, I thought. *I'd never even thought of that as an option.*

Little did I know that, in the not-so-distant future, we would be working on making that happen.

***

Ashes

Michael's remains were cremated, and when the time came to pick up his ashes, I was the one who went to the mortuary. Outside in the parking lot, I took a deep breath and then walked inside. I felt uncomfortable being there, thinking about all the other people who had walked through those doors, all the changes that had happened in their lives.

One of the friendly staff members met me, and I waited until she brought out Michael's ashes in a plain brown plastic box. I signed the paperwork as she put the box in a colorful bag. As I walked back out the door, I looked at the bag I was carrying, felt the weight of it. Questions ran through my head: *Is this all there is? Is this how life ends up, being*

carried out in a shopping bag like a business transaction? What the hell?!
This doesn't seem right.

I got in the car and stared out the front windshield. My hands gripped the steering wheel, yet I was unable to move. As I looked over at the bag, hard feelings of loss, grief, sadness, and anger washed over me.

This isn't right.

At that moment, I felt raw and exposed. I didn't care about all the roles the world tried to put on me, the shoulds, the to-do's. Sitting in my car, I let those emotions run their course through me until I could finally take a breath.

When you're not distracted by the world or pulled in many directions, you become powerful.

***

Snot Cries

I wanted to get out of pain, to stop feeling this grief and guilt about losing Michael. I didn't know what to do with this hurt always lurking just beneath the surface that raised its head at inopportune moments. How was I going to get through this?

Part of the healing process—which was scary and probably necessary, at least for me anyway—involved turning and facing what seemed to be overwhelming: that intense feeling of absolute devastation, of being out of control of my feelings, of feeling lost, of not knowing what would come next. It was important to me to turn and face the situation to whatever degree I could. Not doing so dishonored Michael, myself, and our relationship, and that wasn't going to happen.

When the emotional intensity within yourself is so great, sometimes all you can do is endure and let it run its course.

I've heard it said you have to learn to let things go—that in order to move on, you have to say goodbye. Maybe there's a partial truth there, but that never felt right to me. It makes sense to say goodbye to the things that don't serve you, but not to the person you lost.

I decided that, no matter what, I would do my best to face it, endure it, survive it, move through it, and move with it. This decision tested my beliefs about what was true about life and death. In moments of grief, I didn't care about the price of gas or the latest crisis on TV. My focus was on the questions, "What do I know?" and, "What is real?"

For me, feelings of loss, regret, or failure are sometimes accompanied by what I call "snot cries." Nothing can hold it back. It flows out of my eyes, nose, and mouth, and my body is tense. Something bound up is unraveling. I'm breathing heavily, almost gasping for air. It's like something is trying to move out of my body and, at the same time, trying to move in.

When it subsides, there's a sense of relief. There's space, a small opening to relax. Then the naïve thought comes: *Wow, I'm glad I'm done with that. I don't have to feel that again.* Afterward, I would sometimes think that I didn't care about living or dying—not in the sense of giving up, but more like I could do anything and not care about the outcome.

If you experience this—at some point, when you're ready—revisit that experience and find the gems that are there for you. And they are *for you*, for your benefit, for your well-being. This is not something you have to go back and fix. Take your time; this is not a race. Bring yourself to those situations; bring what you need. The bonds you make within yourself on this internal journey can never be taken away.

Chapter Twenty-Three

Here's Some Advice

Michael rarely asked for things other than rides to see his friends and an occasional video game, so his last wish to have his ashes blasted off in fireworks became my mission. I wasn't exactly sure how it was going to happen, but it wasn't a question of "if"; I knew not doing it wasn't an option.

I started making phone calls, thinking that maybe there was a permit or designated place to do this in our county. Southern California had been experiencing a drought, and I soon discovered it was illegal to even buy a sparkler, let alone obtain the kind of fireworks I was picturing.

I tried for weeks and weeks, talking to city and county officials, wedding planners, graduation coordinators, event planners at golf courses, and even people who manufactured fireworks in other states—anyone who might handle fireworks and be able to point me in the right direction. It was one roadblock after another.

I discovered that putting remains and fireworks together required someone to not only have a license for fireworks and to be bonded and insured, but also to be a mortician licensed to handle remains in the county. It kept getting more and more complicated.

I did find one place that said it may be possible. They coordinated the fireworks for the city and told me I could hire a barge to go out in the ocean, but the cost for the barge was fifteen thousand dollars, not including the fireworks, the permits, the fire department fees, and the manpower to set off the fireworks. That didn't seem very practical. Plus, I wanted something more personal, not something put on for the whole city.

Every day, I became more and more frustrated. How was I going to make this happen? Despite this, my determination and conviction just got stronger. The best way I can describe my inner resolution is this: *Either you can work with me, I go around you, or I go through you, and I don't really care which way it happens.*

As I saw it, there were two paths I could take: one, find a legal way to set off the fireworks; or two, just blast them off, apologize later, and pay whatever fines they may dream up. For the time being, I continued trying the legal way.

I thought I might have better results by making these requests in person, so I was on my way to another golf course to speak to an event planner. I had seen them setting off fireworks there last year, and I was hopeful but still feeling a lot of pressure to get this done.

As I was driving, I felt Michael's presence right beside me. He said, "Hey, Dad, look at where I was when I said it would be fun to be blasted off in fireworks. It was fun, silly, and a little out of the ordinary. If this isn't fun, then just don't do it."

This hit me hard, as it was the first time I'd heard him say anything like this. I felt the intention behind what he was saying. As it sunk in, the tears started coming, and I began to relax a little.

"Okay," I said out loud.

I needed to take a different approach. I was getting too bound up in trying to "make" it happen rather than the spirit behind it.

It somehow reminded me of a Christmas gift Michael had given me when he was nine years old. It's a piece of cardboard with pennies taped on it in the shape of a smile. Next to the smile, it says, "Merry Christmas!!! Here is some advice... Have fun and enjoy yourself today!"

Here is Some Advice

He was wise beyond his years.

After that, I relaxed even more, letting go of some of the pressure I'd put on myself. Little by little, I learned to trust however this was going to unfold.

Later in the day, I received another downloaded message:

Hey, you don't have to do this all on your own. Just put it out there, what you're trying to do, and it will be taken care of.

I decided to follow through on this message. I called a few of my friends to let them know what we were trying to do, and then we sent a text message to Michael's friends letting them know we were looking for fireworks and a spot to blast them off. Five minutes later, they texted back, saying, "Don't worry about the fireworks. We got this. We'll go get them."

I was so impressed by that. Here were these eighteen-year-olds who had the willingness and also the determination to make this happen, even if they had to drive to another state.

I would realize later that all those dead ends and unreturned phone calls were exactly what needed to happen. What I thought of as failure and not trying hard enough was just guiding me toward what turned out to be something far better.

A few days later, after talking it over with my wife and daughter, I decided we would not only have one set of fireworks, but two: one in Michigan with my family and another in California with Michael's friends.

When we thought about where we would launch the Michigan fireworks, the Michigan cabin came to mind first. A two-track dirt road through the forest takes you to the rustic cabin, which sits along a river. There are no neighbors, it's quiet, and you have the place to yourself. We took the kids there as they were growing up to have campfires, make s'mores, swim, inner-tube, and kayak, and with no TV, phone, internet, or running water, the cabin is a beautiful place to unplug and get away. Michael had loved it there; he'd had a lot of fun fishing, making fires, chopping wood, shooting BB guns, and so much more.

As far as where and how we were going to do the fireworks in California, that was yet to be seen.

CHAPTER TWENTY-FOUR

MICHIGAN

We'd planned a trip to Michigan months before Michael passed. I was looking forward to seeing my sister, camping with my dad, and meeting up with three high school buddies I hadn't seen in a long time. But now, it would also be a time to blast off fireworks for Michael's celebration. I didn't want this to be a big get-together; I wanted it to be a private event with just our immediate family to honor Michael and fulfill his wishes.

The plan was to fly in, spend a couple of days with my friends, go camping near Mackinac Island with my dad, and then meet everyone at our cabin for fireworks. It was going to be a fast trip, especially for my wife and Jen, who were flying in from California on the red-eye flight the same day we were doing the fireworks.

Before leaving for Michigan, I needed to track down the fireworks. To my surprise as I looked online, I found multiple specialty fireworks stores available. The closest one was in a small town about two hours away from my dad's house. Michigan had none of the restrictions I had been coming up against in California.

I gave the store a call and happened to get the manager on the phone. I told her I was flying in from California in a few weeks and looking for some fireworks for the celebration of Michael's life.

"Well, we're actually going to be closed then," she said. "It's the end of the season for us. But ya know, I only live a few miles away, and I can come down and meet you at the store when you get in town."

"Wow, that would be great!" I said. "Do you have any fireworks that you would recommend?"

"Well, if you want big ones, that when they go off you can feel the impact in your chest, then I would go with the ones called Juiced Shells."

This was a mortar-style firework that shot out of a tube. The name caught my attention, and they felt like a perfect match to me: first because Michael would like the idea of a bigger explosion, and second because he liked the rapper Juice WRLD.

"Yep, those sound like the ones," I said.

She gave me her cell phone number and told me to give her a call the day before I left so we could arrange a time to meet. I thanked her again and paid for the fireworks online.

The Flight

It was early, 6:00 a.m., when my wife dropped me off at the airport. I had called the airline earlier about transporting Michael's ashes and was told it would be no problem. When I got to the TSA security checkpoint, I had to tell them what was in the brown plastic container. I didn't want them opening it and digging around in there unnecessarily. I'd also brought some paperwork from the funeral home just in case they needed it. The TSA guy looked at me and then went to get his supervisor. As I waited, my attention didn't leave the box. Another TSA security person came over and picked up Michael's ashes, and without saying anything, they started walking away.

"Hey, you're going to bring that back, right?" I asked.

"Yes, sir, we're just going over to another scanning machine. This one won't work."

My focus did not wander. I watched where they went and what they did. I moved out of the line so I could have a continual line of sight on Michael's ashes. I didn't want any screw-ups happening. After a few minutes, they brought back the ashes.

"Here you go, sir. Sorry for your loss," one of the guys said as he handed me back the box.

It's amazing how protective you can feel about certain things.

Friends

The cabin holds a special place for me. It's a kind of sanctuary with a lot of good memories. While there, I can spend my day canoeing, playing games, or just quietly watching bright neon-blue dragonflies.

I looked forward to spending time with my friends from high school at the cabin. Since we were spread out across the United States, it was difficult for us to get together. These were my buddies who I grew up with and had known since middle school. The ones I got in trouble with, made crazy decisions with, and had plenty of close calls. We'd been there for each other when things got tough.

When we arrived, it didn't take long for us to pick up where we'd left off. We played cards, ate junk food, went in the river, shot some pellet guns, and sat around the campfire, reminiscing and catching up on what was going on in our lives. At times, I laughed so hard that tears rolled down my face and my stomach hurt. One of my friends had brought a cornhole game set to donate to the cabin, and we all signed the bottom of the board in honor of Michael. Of course we played a few games, accompanied by some friendly trash-talking. Sure, we were older, but it was as if no time had passed at all.

Surprisingly, our conversations would sometimes turn to religion, which was funny because when we were growing up, religion was the furthest thing from our minds. I still remember getting a Sunday paper route so I wouldn't have to go to Sunday school. We'd built trust in each other over a long period of time, and we knew we could talk about anything.

Spending a few days there offered me a much-needed break. I had time to unplug for a while and just be with friends with no immediate responsibilities. I love these guys, and it reminded me of how precious the time that we spend with other people is, how we don't always have forever to do things together, and that we should take advantage of what really matters when we can.

***

Earlier, I had been asking for a deeper communication with Michael. When I was reflecting on spending time with my friends, Michael jumped in and began telling me about his friends. This is what he shared:

Spending time with your friends, just laughing and having fun—yes, it's like that with my friends. It's the freedom of having fun, being silly, trying new things, without the weight of responsibility and, you should be doing this. I know you can identify with that. This is not about feeling sad or about loss; it's about opening up and exploring a deeper joy, fun, and being. I felt that with my friends, and that's why I love them so much. They are part of me, part of who I am becoming. I reach out to them in many ways, including through you, since you are open.

Michael continued:

We already have that connection and history. You are asking for things you already have, so there isn't the need to put so much effort into this.

Whether on a spiritual or physical level, if you reach out to some of my friends, I will be there in that. I know you can feel the authenticity in what I am saying.

Oh, and I love you too. Continue writing. Those words will be felt and shared with many. Do not give up and be diligent in this. The help is there if you need it. You have nothing to worry about.

CHAPTER TWENTY-FIVE

FIREWORKS

After getting back from the cabin with my friends, my dad and I packed up the fifth-wheel camper trailer, hopped into the extended-cab Chevy truck with the trailer in tow, and headed out for a two-hour ride to pick up the fireworks.

I'd called the store manager earlier to confirm our meeting. It turned out that the store would be open, and she said she would see us there. As we pulled up to the store, there was a sign on the door that said, "Gone for lunch. Be back at 12:15," and another person was waiting as well. When the manager got back, she let us inside. The store had a ton of fireworks. All the aisles and walls were full of colorful packages with strange names like "Agent of Boom," "Little Guru," "Black Mamba Shell," and so on. Of course, how could I tell what these things really were? Certainly not by the name. I felt like I was in the right place.

After finishing up with the other customer, the manager called us over to the counter. She looked my name up on the computer, but there was no record of the purchase. My heart sank a little bit. It wasn't like we could come back in another week or so to pick up this order; we were heading back to California in a few days.

I showed her the printed receipt I'd brought with me, and she checked the computer again with a puzzled look on her face.

"Sorry," she said, "we don't actually have those anymore. Whoever was supposed to put them aside and hold them for us didn't do it, or they got sold. But let's see what we have."

She walked us over to another aisle and grabbed a large box off the shelf. "Here, these are really good."

The three-foot-long box was colorful, printed with all kinds of warnings, and fairly heavy. It was twice the cost of the fireworks I had originally bought. The box read, "Juiced 24 Big-Ass Breaks, 60-Gram Canister Shells." They were mortar-style fireworks, each being about the size of a small soup can, with extra-long fuses.

I looked at my dad and nodded. "These look good."

The manager asked, "Do you want to see some of these same fireworks that were brought back by another customer?"

"Sure."

She took us to a back room. Laid out on the table were the charred, mangled remains of launch tubes and the smell of burnt chemicals. The fireworks had exploded inside the tube without shooting into the air. *Glad I wasn't next to these when they went off*, I thought.

"It's really important to make sure you don't put the canisters in upside down, or this will happen," she said with a smile.

I laughed. "Thanks for the tip."

As we were getting ready to leave, the manager walked over with two small boxes in her hands. "Here, I'd like for you to have these on the house," she said, putting them in my bag.

These fireworks were in the shape of a cube, about twelve inches square. It had one fuse and about sixteen individual fireworks inside, which went off one right after another. I was surprised and grateful for her generosity. I thanked her again, and we headed out the door.

***

My dad and I pulled into the campground. It was right on Lake Huron, and we could see the Mackinac Bridge and Mackinac Island from our camping spot.

We decided to take a ferry over to the island and try a drive-it-yourself horse-and-buggy tour. I like trying new things, because you never know what's going to happen. The buggy was pulled by a single horse that you guided along paved trails around the island. Luckily, our horse, Dan, knew where he was going. I'm not sure what Dan had been eating, but he was pretty gassy. Every time he raised his tail, we knew it wouldn't be good for us, and we could only hold our breath for so long. My dad and I just started laughing because, I mean, what else were we gonna do when we were being farted on by a horse? We spent the rest of our time catching up and seeing other sights in the area.

After we'd headed back home, my dad and I examined the fireworks more closely. The tubes that held the fireworks were a little sketchy; they weren't vertical when sitting on their base and needed some modifications to make them stable. My dad and I built another base for them out of wood to compensate for the tilt. Having grown up on a farm, my dad always had a do-it-yourself attitude, so this wasn't anything out of the ordinary for us.

***

The next day, I went to the airport to pick up my wife and Jen. They had flown in on the red-eye flight and were pretty tired. Luckily, they were able to catch some Zs on our drive back up to the cabin. My dad and sister were already there when we arrived.

I was unloading the car when my wife came over and noticed the label on one of the fireworks. Her eyes got really big when she read, "I GOT THIS," in big letters on the front of the box. This was Michael's expression when he was about to do something for the first time. It was another sign.

I Got This Fireworks

***

After we finished unpacking the food and fireworks, we all went to the spot where Michael first learned how to shoot a BB gun. We stood in a circle, shared how much we loved and missed him, and said our goodbyes. I spread some of his ashes on the ground in the pattern of a gratitude symbol. I shared how Michael, in addition to being my son, is also a teacher of mine. I know it didn't make sense to everyone there, but he has shown me the places where I still need to grow and how to not be so hard on myself. Even after passing, he still reminds me of our connection with life and each other.

After we said our goodbyes, we headed back into the cabin and had a great lunch on the handmade pine table that my grandpa made as we waited for it to get dark.

While unwrapping the fireworks inside the cabin and making sure everything was in order, there was a sense of excitement and anticipation of what was to come. I went back into safety-conscious mode, examining the launch pad that my dad and I had built to rest the tubes on so they wouldn't tip over when ignited. These fireworks would do some serious damage if they went off in any direction other than up.

As we were getting ready, I could feel Michael's presence around me. He was right there. He was so excited. It felt like the energy on Christmas morning when he was young, anxiously waiting to open his presents. He was saying, "Come on! Hurry up! You don't have to do all this safety stuff. Let's just light these." He was so happy.

Outside, my dad, sister, and wife had all set up lawn chairs to watch. On fall nights, Michigan can be chilly. My dad was wrapped up in a blanket, and we all had our jackets on. Jen stood off to the side, ready to video everything using her cell phone. The air was crisp, with a clear sky filled with stars. The feeling was light, and we were all joking around.

Rather than cutting open the fireworks to modify them, I sprinkled some of Michael's ashes on top just before I lit them off. Then I lit the first one. The fuse burned fast, and I ran, not knowing how much time I had to get away. There was a distinct *whoosh* as the fireworks left the launching tube, the inevitable pause as the canister rose higher and higher, and then *boom*. These fireworks didn't disappoint, as everyone who didn't plug their ears for this first one ended up plugging their ears for all that followed. As promised, the fireworks were loud and beautiful. It was great. I asked my wife and everyone else whether they wanted to light one off, but there were no takers.

I felt a sense of completion after the last of the fireworks went off. From my daughter's picture, you could tell that the very last firework was distinct from the others. To me, it looked like an angel. I got the feeling that Michael liked this, especially that we had come together to honor him and his life. It was great that my dad and sister were there as well.

Michigan Fern with Michael's Fireworks

Last Firework

We packed up the cars and headed to my dad's house before going back to California the next morning. We still needed to do another set of fireworks with Michael's friends, but, given all the restrictions, I wasn't sure how that was going to happen.

Chapter Twenty-Six

Finding a Spot

When we arrived home, it was time to focus on the fireworks with Michael's friends. I decided that the desert was our best bet, but I wasn't sure where. The desert is a big place, and it's not easy to tell people, "Hey, just meet us at the third sand dune on the left."

I decided to take a scouting trip out there to see what might be a good fit. This time before leaving, I set an intention to be open, receive, and have a light heart—to find a place that would honor Michael and his friends.

It was a beautiful, sunny Sunday. I started the search at a place we had visited years ago that rented out ATVs. It was always a blast to ride them, and Michael had fun doing donuts and racing around the trails. The quiet drive gave me time to reminisce about my trips out there riding with my son, brother, and daughter. My wife would come on these trips, too, but she was happy just watching; she never rode.

As I exited the freeway onto the local road, I came to a barricade that said, "Road Closed." It was only blocking my lane on this two-lane road, so I eyeballed down the road as far as I could see. I didn't see any major obstacles, so I drove around the barricade and continued driving on the wrong side of the road to where I remembered the quad rental place to be. The road was filled with deep potholes, and large sections were broken and crumbling, requiring me to pay attention to where my tires were tracking.

After a few miles, I pulled up to what looked like a house surrounded by a tall chain-link fence and a gate with a couple of outbuildings. It was miles from anything else, but I was pretty sure this was the place. When I got out of the car, I heard several dogs barking. Inside the open chain-link gate, a couple of guys were repairing quads in the sandy yard. This place felt familiar to me. It reminded me of my dad's garage and machine shop back in Michigan, with all the projects being worked on, the power tools, and the smell of gas and oil. I approached the first guy, whose back was turned to me as he squatted down working on an engine, and said hello.

He didn't look back. Before I could say anything else, he turned his head halfway and said, "If you have any questions, you'll need to talk to the owner," then motioned to one of the outbuildings.

I started walking over, and, before I could get there, the owner came out the garage door and met me. He was probably in his late sixties or early seventies, wore overalls, and had a grease rag in his hand. I didn't recognize him from the time we'd come here before; as it turned out, he had taken over the place just a few years ago. He reminded me of my dad—a good guy, honest and straightforward.

"What can I do for you?" he asked.

"I have a question that maybe you could help me out with. My son recently passed, and it was his last wish to be blasted off in some fireworks. So I was wondering if you knew of any good places for that."

He looked at me and thought for a second. "There's a canyon down the road here a few miles. The bridge is out, but if you stay on the sand trail that goes around the bridge, you can probably make it in a car. Just don't go off the trail or stop, or you'll get stuck in the loose sand. You could also go down this other way," he said, pointing. "There's another canyon, and there's some spots there."

"I really don't know," I said. "Which one do you recommend?"

"How many people will be coming?" he asked.

"My wife and daughter and some of my son's friends. Probably about twelve."

He paused and looked me straight in the eye. "You could do it here if you like," he said, pointing to an area behind his house. The space back there opened up to the trailhead where we rode the quads. He continued, "That way, the women will have a place to go to the bathroom if they need to."

I was surprised by his generous offer. "That would be great. We can pay you for letting us use the place."

"Don't worry about it," he said. "Just let me know when you'd like to come."

He gave me his business card, and I thanked him. Everything had fallen into place. The whole conversation took about five minutes, and our desert location had been set. I was amazed at how open and welcoming the owner was. He didn't know me, yet he offered to let about twelve strangers come over to his home. He had absolutely no concerns about the fireworks; there were none of the restrictions or red tape we'd been dealing with up until that point.

After I got back home, we let Michael's friends know we had a location for the fireworks, then picked a day during the week that wouldn't interfere with the owner's quad rental business. Michael's friends would bring the fireworks they had gotten from out of state.

We sent over the directions, telling them to ignore the "Road Closed" sign.

I didn't know it at the time, but I would be delivering a message from Michael to his friends.

***

Desert Fireworks

I woke up early with a mixture of nervous energy and anticipation. The day of the desert fireworks had finally arrived, and we were meeting with Michael's friends to celebrate his life.

My mind, on the other hand, was filled with questions: *How can I honor Michael? What does it really mean to honor someone? What's the meaning and purpose of all this?* I thought about the ways we typically honor people because of what they achieve, the roles they fulfill, or their personality traits. All of these have judgments attached to them and vary so much from culture to culture. They seemed incomplete to me at best.

Before we left, I was in my home office taking care of a few last-minute work details. My phone, which was lying screen up about a foot away from me, suddenly turned on. There was no ring or vibration, even though I had those settings turned on, and I hadn't touched my phone in over an hour. When I looked over at the screen, I saw Michael's picture—the one that would show up when I received a text or call from him.

This got to me, and I could feel his presence in the room. He was right there, reminding me that he wasn't really gone. "Hey, Michael. I'm glad you're here," I said out loud.

The funny thing is, this exact same situation happened to my wife months later after she asked Michael to let her know he was still here.

My wife, my daughter, her boyfriend, and I all took one car to meet at the quad rental location. It was about an hour before sunset when we parked in front of the closed chain-link gate. I stepped out of the car but didn't see anyone around. The air was warm and dry, the clear sky was dotted by a few clouds, and the dogs were barking, announcing our arrival.

After a short wait, the owner came out. "Hi, I almost forgot that you were coming. Is this all of you?"

"No," I replied, "we have a few more cars coming."

"My wife and I would like to get all of you some pizza," the owner said.

"I really appreciate that, but we're good. I appreciate you letting us do this here."

He offered a few more times, but I politely declined each time. I didn't want to complicate what we were doing by bringing pizza into the mix.

Two carloads of Michael's friends arrived a few minutes before dark, but we were still waiting for one more car to come. They were having a hard time finding the place. When they finally arrived, Michael's friends all laughed and dogged on them, I guess because it wasn't unusual for them to get lost. Unfortunately, Google Maps had taken them to the wrong location.

It was dark when the owner opened the gate to let us in and headed back into his house. We walked out into the desert, bringing a shovel just in case we needed it. Michael's friends were laughing and joking around, telling stories about all the crazy stuff Michael would do and how he would always make them laugh, how they were amazed at all the things he would make. I recognized, then, that all the locations I had tried to arrange for the fireworks, all the frustrating denials and dead ends, would have led to a location that was too restrictive, too formal for his friends. This was the perfect space for them to just be themselves.

Before we blasted off the fireworks, I shared how Michael had been showing us signs of being here, like the .50-caliber rubber bullet on my desk and the picture on my phone. They smiled and said, "Yup, that sounds like Michael."

I told them that he was still here with us and that if they ever wanted to talk with him, they could. I got the feeling that this was important for them to hear, that Michael wanted to let them know.

I sprinkled Michael's ashes on top of the fireworks, then we lit them off. They were spectacular. One person brought firecrackers, and his friends all chased each other around with them and laughed. They asked me if I wanted to throw some firecrackers, so I joined in.

I hadn't known Michael's friends very well, since they hadn't spent a lot of time at our house. As I watched them talking with each other, joking around, and having fun, I saw how close they were to each other. I thought about all the adventures and experiences they had already gone through in their young lives. It was beautiful, and it reminded me of my friends when we were their age, just experiencing life—the kind of friends that you could just be crazy and have fun with. I saw how Michael fit in with them, the bond of friendship they'd had, and, in so many ways, how he added to their lives. It occurred to me that maybe I'd been guided to see this. I got the sense that Michael was sharing this with me, and in that moment I was a part of it, too. It was his way of showing and sharing his love with me. I felt so fortunate and blessed to be able to see this firsthand. When someone shares what they love with you, it reflects how they feel about you.

And as for those questions in my mind, I stopped looking for the meaning of things. It felt more open and authentic to recognize and honor Michael as a spirit on his journey. Seeing his spirit in relation to his friends reminded me that underneath all the challenges and struggles, this spark of Life comes forth and expresses itself.

***

A few days later, I got a call from an intuitive friend of mine. She and her husband had just returned from a getaway to the desert to see an air show, and she wanted to share an experience she'd had with Michael. She asked me if we had gone out to the desert yet, and I told her we'd just gotten back a few days ago. She knew I was going, but I hadn't told her when. It turned out that they were in the desert the same day we were. She said Michael came to visit her that day, and he was excited, bouncing all over. He was filling the whole sky with colors and excitement, waiting to be with his friends that night.

CHAPTER TWENTY-SEVEN

YOSEMITE NATIONAL PARK

Yosemite invites you to look up. Tall granite peaks force the eyes up and away from yourself. Its beauty connects and reminds you that you're part of something bigger. It invites you to explore and asks different parts of you to come out and play. Slowing down, you recognize what has been hidden by the busyness of your days and know that there is always another path. It's not the photos you take that last when you leave Yosemite; it's something else that endures, that changes you—a reminder of innocence, beauty, and power that is pure.

***

When the alarm went off at 4:30 a.m., I rolled out of bed and woke up Jen. My wife was staying home this time because of work, so only my daughter and her boyfriend were heading up to Yosemite National Park with me for a few days. We had been planning this trip for months. I love this park, and I was excited about going. Jen said she didn't remember going before, maybe because she had been too young.

We picked up my daughter's boyfriend on the way for his first trip to Yosemite. I hadn't spent much time with him, so I was looking forward to getting to know him better.

We usually did tent camping, but since it was almost November, I decided to splurge and put us up in one of the lodges in the park. I was glad we stayed there. It gets pretty cold at night, and unless you have the right gear, it can be downright uncomfortable.

***

Yosemite Walk

I woke up early, just as the sun was coming up. Jen and her boyfriend were still sleeping, so I went out for an early walk, quietly closing the door to our room so as to not wake them up. Thankfully, the lodge was close to a lot of trailheads and waterfalls. I decided to go to Yosemite Falls only a short distance away.

I felt the crispness of the air as I took a breath in through my nose and saw my breath as I exhaled. It was invigorating—the fall colors mixed with the green of the pine trees against the blue sky, the sun on my face. Off in the distance, I could hear the waterfall. Dry leaves cracked under my feet as I made my way through the parking area toward the trailhead.

I looked up at the granite walls, which had been carved out by glaciers, rising thousands of feet into the air from the valley floor. The sun breaking over the peaks cast its light on the walls and highlighted the shadows on the rock face. I could see the 2,425-foot waterfall in the distance, one of the tallest waterfalls in North America. I had the sense that something special was going to happen.

A couple was standing in the middle of the parking lot with their son. He looked like he was about fifteen years old. They stood close together, turning slowly, pointing to all the beautiful sights, smiling and laughing. My throat tightened, and an overwhelming feeling of sadness came over me. I felt the loss of Michael more sharply, and the tears started coming.

As I took a few deep breaths and continued walking toward the falls, I was shown images of what I can only describe as the Native American Indians that used to live in this Valley. I could feel their presence, a sacredness, and their deep respect for nature and our place in it. It was a familiar feeling. I had the sense that we'd met before, and I felt welcomed to be here, taken care of, and nurtured.

I took a different path to the falls, one that wasn't paved or marked with signs. This trail was quieter, softer. It allowed me to go slowly, to notice more, to breathe in the smells of the trees and earth. I kept moving, climbing over the boulders that had fallen from the granite wall. Pine needles cushioned my footsteps as the sound of water hitting the rocks got louder and louder.

Thoughts about work and other things would pop into my head, but they were totally out of place—not what I wanted to be thinking about. I asked myself what, if anything, I could do to stop them. In my mind's eye, I saw that I could just move them to an area behind me, out of my awareness, if I wanted. I didn't have to try to get rid of the thoughts, fix them, or shield myself from them; I just had to move them behind me, out of sight. After I did this, everything opened up. I was more fully there. All the colors around me were more vibrant, and I felt more alive and free.

At the base of the falls, spray and mist were showering me. I made my way over to a small tree that let me get close without getting too wet. The early morning sun was causing rainbows to form in the mist, painting beautiful patterns of light as the water danced in the wind along the rocks. I was surrounded by beauty, sunshine, rainbows, mist, the sound of water flowing, and, at the same time, sadness. It was all happening at once, all connected and okay.

I started a conversation with Michael, telling him I was glad he was here and that I was sorry I didn't give him more love and support when he was here physically.

His message came back: "You know that's just crazy, right?"

"Yeah, I know," I said out loud, "but it's the feeling I have."

The mist and spray were coming down stronger now. At the top of the waterfall, the water was flowing over the edge in a steady stream. It seemed whole, but as I watched it fall, it began to break up, becoming smaller and smaller. The wind blew it in new directions, taking it along a different path than where it started, until the water finally landed on the rocks below, only to eventually come back together and continue its journey down the stream.

Maybe I'm like the water that's flowing over the edge of the cliff, I thought. *As I fall, I begin to scatter and get blown around by the wind. I get broken down and hit the rocks below, and then slowly settle and come back together to continue on my journey.*

Yosemite Falls

After spending more time there, I began making my way back. I felt more open and lighter, and, again, I felt the presence of the Native Americans with me as I walked.

Soon, I felt strongly drawn to a tree, a sequoia. Its trunk was about six feet in diameter with rough, deep grooves. It had a split at the base in the shape of an upside-down V. I can't really describe it other than to say I felt a connection to this tree. As I stood in front of it, I became aware of its life, that it had been here for a very long time, growing through many cold winters and hot summers, droughts, and fires, and that it was where it was supposed to be. I felt a sense of respect, that it was able to endure and thrive in these situations. The air was still as I moved closer. I put my hand on the reddish-brown trunk; the bark was rough and dry. For the first time, my eyes traveled up the tree trunk to find that all the branches were dead, though you wouldn't know it from looking at the base of the trunk. I didn't feel sadness when seeing this, just respect and recognition that it was continuing on its life cycle. I recognized that this tree wasn't diminished by death in any way; it was still a tree, beautiful in a different way. I felt the timelessness of this moment, how things fit together, how they also pulled apart, and the beauty that was within it all. My heart felt welcomed in this space, and I didn't want to leave, so I stayed there for a while, letting this feeling of everything being okay and in its place soak in.

Sequoia Tree

My daughter and her boyfriend would be waking up soon, so I decided I should probably get back. When I returned to the lodge, they were just waking up. I didn't share all the things I had experienced that morning. I was focused on grabbing some breakfast with them and starting the day, getting ready for the next adventure.

***

After Michael's passing, going on walks was helpful for me. It got me out of the house and took me out of my head. You may discover going to your own getaway place to be helpful. It doesn't have to be Yosemite, but a place in nature near you where there are few distractions—a private place you can go to reconnect with your inner self and Spirit. Invite your loved one to join you if you like. Go slow and take your time. Say hello, listen, and honor where you are at. This is not a race trying to reach a destination. May you find your own Yosemite that brings connection with your loved one.

Chapter Twenty-Eight

Meeting Loss and Death

Loss feels like something is being torn away. It's not gentle. But what is being torn?

Loss is vast and deep, it appears throughout time, and it can be subtle or overwhelming. Death seems finite, yet it too is infinite. Pain shows us where we're hanging on to our judgments and expectations—our judgment about what was lost, and our expectations about we will be missing in the future. It's these judgments and expectations that hold things in place.

Loss is not fixed; loss is energy shifting. And death and life are the same thing.

What I know is that the heart is not limited in any way; it is not restricted by time or death. When your heart desires connection with someone you have lost, it is available to you without restrictions in a way that matters. In this tearing down of loss and death, there is a hidden gift.

***

Meeting Michael

I began letting go of my judgments and expectations of Michael. It challenged the memories I held, the ones I tried to make meaning of events, determine value, and see things as right and wrong. The more I released those judgments, the more it shook the foundation of my beliefs about how things are.

When my judgments, expectations, and desires were stripped away, what was left was the essence of Michael, who he truly is—not what he had done or could have done, not what he'd achieved or didn't accomplish. But his essence and presence of who he is and continues to be.

***

I met Michael's pure presence. There was just joy, being, and complete wholeness in that moment. I experienced the most intimate sharing of myself—authentic, raw, exposed, enveloped in love. Nothing was lacking. I didn't have to hold anything back; I brought everything to that moment, all of me.

That essence, or presence, does not go away; it transcends time. It cannot be lost or taken away. When you meet with someone in that expansive space, embracing one another, honoring each other, and feeling gratitude, you become richer. In that meeting, you can go as deep as you like. In that intimate space, there are no barriers; you see each other as the beautiful beings you are. Love bathes in this space, and no words are necessary.

What a gift it is to be shown Michael's presence on this level, to experience a sharing, a fellowship, an honoring—to know what is and what is possible. This is where freedom is: in a relationship, with Michael and with everyone. How beautiful! None of this could have taken place without the foundation of love that is present here. Sharing that most intimate space is truly all that matters.

Michael, thank you for sharing your presence, being with me, and sharing your blessings and light. My life is richer because of you, which is infinitely valuable.

My experience with loss and grief continues to go deeper and deeper, ever-expanding, revealing its beauty and love. I'm humbled and grateful to be shown what is offered; the heart behind it is rich and deep. This is meeting death with much havingness and love. This is meeting death as Life.

CHAPTER TWENTY-NINE

REFLECTIONS

Grief and Sadness

When grief and sadness touch you, or you touch grief and sadness in another person, anything that matches those feelings is also there. It's not just the grief of a particular event but other events as well that get triggered within you. It's as if you carry around dormant feelings, and when you touch those emotions, it brings them alive, wakes them up, and brings them to the surface. Michael's passing brought a lot of things to the surface with an intensity that wasn't easy to stuff down or push aside: my beliefs, judgments of myself and others, how things are supposed to be, and how life is to be lived.

So what's the point? What's the reason? Maybe it's to allow an opportunity for unresolved wounds to be healed. Maybe it's to relive the feelings, to remember something, or to hold onto a belief. Maybe those feelings are coming up because you're ready to release them. Maybe you're watching them and feeling them as they leave.

It's like when you have a good cry. Afterward, you feel physically spent and tired, but somehow cleansed, lighter, like there's a new space within yourself, and you can breathe a little more easily. Sometimes we need a good clearing out.

It can be, and is, an incredible opportunity to forgive. Forgive yourself for your believed failures. Forgive your child for the things they did and did not do. Moving in the direction of forgiveness strips away those things that separate us from ourselves, bringing us toward acceptance and unconditional love—not as a way to just cover our hurts, but to help us authentically approach our inner self with compassion and understanding. To allow ourselves to move toward loving ourselves for what we truly are.

As reasons and judgments fall away, there is more space to breathe, more freedom to choose how we want to live our lives, and more of what we value and what is important to us. Michael's passing brought all that grief, sadness, judgment, and anger to the surface and allowed me to see things more deeply within myself. From there, I was able to work with and heal some of these aspects, which ultimately moved me toward a better life.

Relationships change, and my relationship with Michael continues to evolve and grow in new ways. If someone had told me in the beginning that Michael's death was an opportunity, a kind of blessing, I would probably have said they were full of s***. It doesn't always feel like a blessing to me, but I know that it is, and one way I can honor Michael and myself is to not let this opportunity be wasted. So I choose to live with the opportunity Michael has given me—all the tears, pain, sadness, laughter, depth, beauty, and love.

***

Letting Go

You invest a lot in your kids: your time, love, goals, desires, and hope for how things will turn out for them. When they pass, those dreams are still there, but now with no person to attach them to or build them with. You never know how that is going to unravel for you.

I went to our credit union to close Michael's accounts. I had the forms they required, a death certificate, and a signed affidavit that probate wasn't required. As I sat there, I could feel the grief beginning to well up in me. My throat tightened, and I fought back the tears. I realized how much this bank account represented, not about how much money he had, but his future and his independence. Michael was way more of a spender than a saver. Still, it was just one step toward him becoming an independent person, and now it wouldn't be there anymore. I started to get angry. *What good is this money?* I thought. *All this focus on money when it doesn't mean s***.*

As I drove away from the bank, these feelings subsided. I reminded myself to be compassionate, to give myself a little more space, to breathe.

This unraveling, this letting go, is unpredictable at best. I noticed if something kept recurring, I had a big part in it. I wasn't willing to let something go. For me, letting go doesn't mean getting rid of something; it means letting it be and not feeling like I have to try to fix it. Meeting and accepting what is.

I noticed that part of me liked the intensity those memories and judgments brought with them. I liked the highs and lows; they made me feel alive instead of numb. But I also noticed my belief that if I didn't feel something intensely, it somehow meant I didn't care about it or didn't care about Michael. I know from experience that is not true. Instead, when I can be more accepting and neutral toward my feelings, I can go deeper. My initial reactions occur on the surface, and when I have the presence to honor them and myself, I experience more space and the freedom of choice. I'm free to move closer, to be more intimate, share more deeply, to say, "I love you," from a more authentic space, rather than trying to prove or maintain a certain way of being.

***

Judgments

Judgments feel real and solid. They are backed up with "facts," yet when you see them for what they are, change is possible. As I began releasing judgments of myself and Michael, a shift happened: a space was created for forgiveness and gratitude.

Over time, I gradually moved from saying, "I forgive myself for not doing this," or, "I forgive him for doing that," to what felt like a hug, an embrace with no edges. This embrace I'm speaking of is not so much about forgiving specific things or being grateful; it's about being gratitude itself, forgiveness itself. It includes everything. A presence within you that requires no effort and is not tied to an outcome.

CHAPTER THIRTY

DOWNLOADED MESSAGES FROM SPIRIT

Downloads are messages I receive from Spirit and I write them down as I receive them. I know they are for me, but you may find some benefit as well.

Forgiveness

Forgiveness is about an embrace, a hug; it comes from the center of your being. When you embrace the center of another in forgiveness, all of time, all the past, all the future is brought into the present moment and held. All things are there, along with all possibilities, nothing is held back.

***

Filling Your Space

Don't be so hard on yourself. Now is not the time for that. No one can be a bigger critic of you than you. You know all your secrets, your vulnerabilities, your weaknesses, and how to reach them. Being hard on yourself is in your mind. It's not generated from your spirit or your essence.

Being hard on yourself causes you to stop, to shrink. Stopping can be good for self-reflection and seeing the bigger picture, but being hard on yourself doesn't come from you and isn't your friend. Don't feed it or fight with it. Any games you play in your mind will ultimately run you around in endless circles.

The better path is to look in the direction you would like to go. Create a little space for yourself, no matter how small, and start by doing one small thing.

I once heard that if you want to shift your perspective, just look up. Yes, physically look up. It sounds strange, but it works.

Of course, there is a hole in your life. You miss your loved one; it's not the same. But as the situation settles down, you get to choose what you fill that hole with. You decide what energy and meaning you will build around, beside, and within that hole. I choose Spirit and honoring because, ultimately, that is what is.

When you give yourself a little space and permission, you can fill that space with whatever you would like in the moment. It can be support, joy, or maybe laughter. Maybe you'll fill that space with abundance, health, happiness, or freedom. But whatever you fill it with, let it be done with kindness for yourself, in a caring, loving way.

You only have so much time here. Do the things you wish to do. See the beauty and listen to the sounds. Feel the air and sun on your skin. Breathe. The less you filter, the more alive you will feel. The length of time you have is not important; the depth to which you can receive is. Recognize that we are all on our own journeys, growing and learning what we need. You cannot mess this up. There is no mistake, for every experience builds on the other, and you either grow deeper or broader.

***

Give to Yourself

Give to your human self what it needs or is even afraid to ask for. When you bring yourself and Love to the situation of loss, you aren't just bringing you there; you're bringing all of your lineage, your spirit guides, your helpers, healers, angels, masters, and other beings throughout and beyond time. Any healing or forgiveness that happens is not just for you, as it ripples outward with amazing power and Grace through the infinite realms within and beyond time. You are so precious. You have no idea how what you're doing now benefits so many. Even though you get glimpses of it, it is beyond your imagination. From that centered space, all is shared. You are doing so well.

***

Choose to See

You are moving from seeing Michael as someone struggling with a problem to the eternal being he is. He is a master—big, beautiful, full of life and joy, funny. You asked for a deeper relationship with Michael, which means your views and filters must be released. You do not have to get rid of anything, only shift where you are viewing, and you do that by actually being that. Be in that space first and then look from there. This is not a mental exercise that tries to get you to someplace that you are not. You are doing so well. These are just gentle reminders for you.

How you choose to see Michael, or anyone for that matter, determines how you feel. Actually, that's not entirely accurate; it's more like where you feel it from. As your human self with edges, you feel things deeply. You feel them in your body. The bigger you are, the more space you have, the more you can be the eternal being you are, the more you can have, the deeper you can go. There is no fear that you will be totally taken over or lost. That infinite, eternal aspect of you already knows it is indestructible and that you never die. That you are free. That you can have a multitude of emotions and thoughts at the same time, and it is not a problem. Remember, you are not trying to fix something or learn the magic technique that solves problems. You are here to bring you, the divided aspects of yourself, to You. Include them with you to honor them as you, like the biggest hug in the world. As you know, the tighter you are hugged by God, the more open and free you feel—free to be yourself.

Express yourself. Honor yourself. Honor others' journeys and choices. Share that; embody that. It is no longer just an idea.

***

Only You

Only you can honor yourself as only you can.

Only you can honor your journey in a way that is uniquely yours.

Only you can give what you need to yourself in the most intimate way.

They are all there for you, waiting to be released for you.

***

Be Kind

When you need to take a break, take a break. When you need to cry, cry. When you need to laugh and do nothing, do that. This is not a race; you do not have to meet a deadline. Be gentle with yourself, be kind, and cut yourself some slack. Be okay with doing nothing, accomplishing nothing, being nothing.

***

You Don't Have to Go Anywhere

You don't have to go anywhere or travel to exotic countries (though that would be fun) to have profound experiences of connection with yourself, with others, and with the universe. These experiences are there for you to access any time you like. They are always available.

Sometimes, when you go searching for something, it's the trying so hard that actually gets in the way of finding it. Often, it's when you're not looking, when you give up the searching, that you'll have the most profound experiences.

***

Don't Be So Hard on Yourself

Don't put the weight of the world on your shoulders. Don't be so hard on yourself. You don't have to do that. Love is not earned or won. You don't earn what is already there. It's just your perception and the judgments you have that allow you to have it. You deserve it. Love is already here and offered freely.

***

Say Hello

How do you communicate with your loved ones? You go internally to where they are—not a physical location, but where their presence is. This is an open, neutral space that's difficult to label. Then you say hello to them, just as an acknowledgment with no agenda. It's a receptive space. That hello can then rest in the space that is everything, including your loved one. In this space, there is room for everything and everyone, and it is beautiful.

***

Love Is Free to Move

Love is free to move. It is not constricted by space, time, life, death, or anything else. It is the connection point that allows you to be with anyone in the past, present, future, and even beyond death. A purity of heart allows for this freedom; it is the central connection point of all things, and therefore, there are no restrictions. Love can be any size—immensely vast with no edges, or as tiny and infinitesimal as you like. You can go anywhere and be anything in Love. It is your freedom. It is You.

***

Healing

When you're healing, when you're releasing things within yourself and especially in relationship with other people, remember that your experiences (even though they're hard) are there for your benefit. Remember to honor the greater whole and see that release as being transmuted and healed to completion. Know that it is for the benefit of all, that the conflict was there to help you as well as others on their journeys. Envelop the experience in love, and honor yourself. These are not failures you are getting rid of or trying to heal. They're not punishments. They are the most direct and caring way for you.

***

Healing the Undesirable

When something undesirable or horrific happens, and you encounter things you want to push away, for true healing to happen, you have to recognize that there is no judgment in healing. How can this be possible? It's possible because where the healing comes from is a place that has only love and honoring. There is no judgment in that space as you view events, people, and things. When you view from this perspective and see from a heart-centered space, you recognize that things are only here to benefit you, to love you, to honor you, to facilitate your growth and your expansion and your possibilities. From this heart-centered space, you are not divided; you are whole and innocent, no matter what is being presented to you. You see what no longer serves you and is not truly an extension of you. You see what is not true, what is not part of you, and since you see that it is not part of who you are, you don't have to hang onto it. You don't have to try to control it. It has no power over you. You are willing to let it go, to let it be, to let it heal. You are doing so well.

Acceptance

You Are Never Alone

When you are on your path, you are never really alone. There are those that you share the path with, those who guide you, and those who explore with you. You are not on this journey by yourself.

One way to see if you are "on track" is whether you feel isolated and alone. If you do, there's a good chance that you're looking in the wrong direction. Even though you are not alone there, either, it may feel like you are. Instead, change what you're looking at. Honor and recognize those on the journey with you, both physically and spiritually.

One thing that helped me when I felt isolated: I would center myself, and set the intention to become aware of all the other people who felt the same way that I felt at that moment, that same aloneness. This may seem counterintuitive, but in doing this, you can recognize that you're not alone, as many other people feel the same way you do. Send them a hello, send them a blessing, and offer your support to them.

CHAPTER THIRTY-ONE

GUIDANCE

Death Is a Teacher

Death is a teacher showing you what you're hanging on to. It's purifying, in a way, shedding those things that are more external and allowing you to see what's left: the heart and center of what is. Death teaches us to look within at what's important to us, the essence of our relationships with those we love. If we look, we'll see the timelessness of what is already here and does not fade. This is invaluable because death has the potential to reveal something about ourselves that may not always be easily seen.

I can honestly say that I feel closer to Michael now more than ever, in part because of what I was able to let go, but even more so because of what I was able to let in.

***

Fill Your Bath

Healing is not usually a one-time event; at least, it hasn't been for me. Emotional healing needs to be revisited. It takes time. It's like gently soaking in a warm bath. Gradually, the warm water slowly relaxes and softens all those aches and pains, especially the places where you've been bracing against yourself or others. When you soften, relax, loosen your grip on what you're hanging on to, then you can finally take a breath. Change happens more easily from this space.

You get to choose what to fill your bath with. But how do you do that? How do you get to that point? How do you choose what to fill your tub with?

I felt a heavy sadness one morning, missing Michael. I was looking on YouTube and found a video by Matt Kahn titled "Dissolving Sadness." I listened to him talk about difficult situations and our relationship to gratitude. One of the things he said struck me: "Thank you for blessing my life and making me better than before you entered."

I stopped the video and let those words sink in. I felt each of those words in relationship to Michael, and I spoke them out loud to both myself and Michael: "Thank you for blessing my life and making me better than before you entered."

Gratitude washed over me, filling those places of hurt and conflict. I slowly repeated this statement until gratitude was all I felt. There was no room for sadness. I stayed with that feeling, letting it move where it wanted to go, letting it fill me. I recognized that the more I allowed this, and spent time with it, the more I experienced a reset in how I felt.

Later, I reflected on what made this so powerful. Was it the gratitude? Yes, but there was something else. I recognized that I could connect 100 percent with this declaration. I wasn't conflicted about it. I had been blessed by Michael being in my life, and, yes, Michael definitely made me a better person. There was no doubt about that. When I coupled that certainty with something as infinite as gratitude, it truly was powerful.

So, again, how do you get there? What can you connect with 100 percent? If you're divided and conflicted about something, if it always seems to flip-flop and change, it's hard to know where you stand in relationship to it.

To find what is real and true for you, to find something you can say yes to absolutely, you have to go a little deeper, which means simpler. (This is the key to healing: being authentic about who you are and where you're coming from.) Once you give your attention to that, to connect with and allow yourself to rest in it, in that moment you will recognize you're already whole and nothing else is needed.

"Thank you for coming into my life and making me a better person," is something I can absolutely, 100 percent get behind, be connected with, and allow to be.

Healing is not about trying to get past something, overcome something, or fix something; healing is about becoming whole. You heal by being whole first, and then, if you choose, you can take action from there.

***

Open or Closed

One day when I felt stressed out, I decided to go see a movie. I asked to be open and aware of anything Spirit would like to show me. At one point in the movie, the main character was fighting against a superior foe. He was punching hard with his fists closed, trying his best, but he had run up against his limitations. Later, he asked his teacher how he could win against this enemy. His teacher showed him that, instead of using a closed fist and trying so hard, he could open his hand and remember who he is. That was all I needed to see: a reminder to open to who I am.

***

Here's the Difference

Here's the difference: When you try to fix things on the outside, try to change conditions to make them better, fix problems in order to make your life easier or to feel better, you are working from the outside in. When, on the other hand, you are connected with Spirit and aligned with your true self, and you encounter the conditions and experiences that you want to change, meeting them from within yourself, there's no expectation of change—and yet they do, without you wanting them to.

***

Embrace Yourself

As much as you miss and want to embrace your loved one, that's how much you need to embrace yourself. Honor yourself. Love yourself. This is one of the best ways to honor them, their memory, and where they are now. As much as you want to hear from them, they want to reach out to you and connect with you on a heart level. Meet them in a place of forgiveness, recognizing each other in an even deeper way than when they were here physically.

***

How to Help

You've probably tried to help someone you care about with a difficult situation. You may have had good advice to offer, but when you shared it with them, it just bounced off, or they couldn't fully take it in.

In Spirit, communication is instantaneous. It's a vibration that each person recognizes, and it doesn't feel like it's coming from outside themselves. This is what allows someone to receive the communication and open up to more possibilities. It's not so much about giving them an answer to a specific problem; it's about a particular energy that opens up the realm of possibilities for that person. It allows them to see what's in front of them, behind them, beside, above, and below. There's a sense of freedom and empowerment that happens automatically when you share something spirit to spirit. There's no element of trying to control, manipulate an outcome, or achieve a certain goal. Instead, you can honor that person's journey, encourage them, and validate their power, position, and experience. You can recognize their human side while at the same time honoring their spirit. In Spirit, there is already oneness.

Trying to take over somebody's responsibility for their journey is very silly. It made me laugh when I saw myself trying to do this in my relationship with Michael. I had been trying to cushion the blows, save him from pain, and make his life as easy as possible. I did this all from the heart of a parent; no one wants to see their kids get hurt. This was, in part, how I was able to begin shifting my inner world concerning Michael's death and releasing that feeling of responsibility, that I had somehow failed him as a parent. This was also how I expanded my awareness to see the bigger picture of myself and Michael on this journey. I could actually see that everything was in alignment and unfolding as it should.

You may ask, how do you help somebody? What are you responsible for? First, set down your own boulders—the boulders you carry when you're trying to make something happen. You don't even have to know what those boulders are. Just set them aside, release them, and wait. Ask for a pure motivation.

When you see the person you're trying to help, where are you? Where are you trying to help them from? Do you see them as just one person? They're actually much more than that. If you only see them as an individual struggling, how do you know what they're here to learn and benefit from? They're much more than just their individual experiences here, and so are you. Clear the space between you. Honor them on their journey. Honor the spirit that you are, knowing that the same spirit that has your back has also been guiding them. So if you just jump in on your own and try to fix something, thinking it's the best thing to do, it may not be aligned with what the Universe has in mind. It may not align with their purpose or what they're trying to accomplish in alignment with their soul.

If you first align with that space within yourself and then see them as being on their own journey in connection with Spirit, it changes where you come from. It changes your relationship with them. Now, when you ask, "How can I truly help this person?", the insights you receive, will be much more aligned with what is truly a match for them. From there, when you ask or offer something, it won't just come from you as a person, but in connection with Spirit.

This is not something somebody can tell you, or be convinced of through a logical explanation that your mind can accept. You have to experience it for yourself. I can, at best, only point towards it. Trying to take over someone's life, control them, or manipulate them is very silly. You can't take over the Universe's job.

This doesn't mean we should just sit back, not do anything, and let life happen. Instead, when we move to the center of our being and then ask how we can help, the answers we receive will be more genuine, filled with energy, beauty, and timelessness. From this centered position, you may find there is no question of what to do. This space is filled with grace and ease automatically. You don't have to figure out what to do; it's already part of you. The inspired actions that follow will be extensions of yourself. It may feel like you're not even trying to do them, yet everything is supported—yourself included—in whatever unfolds.

***

Love the Parts You Don't Like

To have a closer relationship with your loved one, you have to be able to love the parts you don't like.

In a dream, I was sitting at a table with Michael. He was wearing his hoodie and facing about forty-five degrees away from me. This was the part of me that saw him as being disconnected, the judgment that he had a problem. In that moment, I brought love, honoring, and blessings to him. Afterward, I felt more open, loving, and giving. I was then able to hug those parts of myself and Michael that I didn't want to see.

***

Questions

When Michael passed, I became more focused on questions about life and death. I had my own ideas and beliefs, but what did I really know? Asking questions, whether of myself or of Spirit, was invaluable, because it allowed me to experience the answers directly.

The intensity of grief generates an emotional opportunity. As things are being stripped away from you, it's chaotic, but within that intensity is the possibility to go within and see what remains. What falls away? What doesn't change? It's powerful to direct your energy and attention in this way; it allows you to experience what you wouldn't usually experience in everyday life—to see for yourself what is real.

It's not necessary to have emotional intensity to receive these answers, but it can bring a powerful focus to your questions.

I've learned to pay attention to where I'm asking questions from. This is just as important as the questions I ask. If I ask a question while angry, I'll receive an answer filtered through anger. If I ask a question from worry, what will show up will be filtered through worry. If I'm centered and neutral, the answers will have more room to come in and won't necessarily have to fit a preconceived idea.

No matter what emotional space you ask questions from, you can gain insight. The answer, your awareness of it, will meet you where you are.

CHAPTER THIRTY-TWO

IT IS A GIFT

I asked myself: What gifts are being given in this situation?

This is an opportunity to lovingly see where you are at and to reexamine more deeply your relationships and life.

It's a reminder that you're alive, that each person has their own unique journey. It's showing you acceptance, for yourself and others.

It's opening you to a deeper self-love. It's teaching you that you can support yourself in a way that you didn't know you could. You do this by giving yourself the space and permission to get in touch with a feeling of support and then resting in that. Take the time to just be there, not rushing to move on to the next thing.

It's about recognizing that sharing this, in the form of a book, is actually an honor that you're participating in, a way to be of service.

It's about learning and growing. It's teaching you about life and life after death.

It has deepened my relationships with Michael, my wife, my daughter, my sister, my dad, and my friends. I have more appreciation and respect for them.

This situation has allowed me to see where I'm being hard on myself and closing myself off to love.

It has shown me how communities come together and support each other in times of need.

I've recognized and felt more deeply that the Universe is always, always, always watching out for me, taking care of me, working together with me. Even when, and often when, I can't see it.

It has challenged my beliefs about what life is, changing what I view as real and possible.

It has allowed me to ask different questions of myself and the Universe that I never would have otherwise. For example, what's my responsibility to others and myself? What does it mean to be authentic?

It requires me to be even more honest with myself, to look at my shortcomings and see what I could do differently.

It allows me to focus more on the connections that are here instead of just physically doing things.

It has absolutely changed my relationship with Michael. I've moved from being his parent to something more. It is a gift.

***

Michael, you always said "I got this, I got this" when things were tough. It was something that I couldn't believe 100 percent when you were here. I was so worried.

But I'm with you now, and I say with Love, "Michael, you got this... You got this..."

***

My relationship with Michael continues to deepen, and I can't wait to see where it goes next. The signs, dreams, and bullets are always there, and no matter how you communicate with your loved ones, whether through signs, dreams, bullets, or another way, may you be blessed on your journey.

In Loving Memory of
Michael Yuji Abbott
5/24/2002 - 7/20/2021

ABOUT THE AUTHOR

Jeff M. Abbott grew up in the Michigan and currently lives with his wife, daughter and rescue dog in southern California. He loves the outdoors and adventure traveling.

Website: www.jeffmabbott.com

If you enjoyed reading 'Signs, Dreams, and Bullets,' please consider leaving a comment on Amazon or other online bookstore. Your feedback is invaluable and helps other readers discover this story.

Artwork by Jennifer Corra, of Crescent Moon Archives

Afterword

https://jeffmabbott.com

Website

Scan the QR code to listen to "No Cosmic Coincidences" written by Jennifer Abbott on YouTube.